EDITOR'S FOREWORD

Today priests in continuing education, Sisters on renewal weeks, leaders of charismatic prayer groups, and people in parishes bombard the Scripture scholar with the plea: give us more Scripture. They echo the conviction of St. Jerome: ignorance of Scripture is ignorance of Christ.

In our on-going series Herald Biblical Booklets, which was inaugurated two years ago, we tried to meet this plea with popular, inexpensive studies on biblical books and themes. This series has been graciously received. The time seems ripe to introduce a tandem series which will further meet the needs of the people of God by exploring in a thoroughgoing way the relationships of the Bible to daily life and to prayer. This new series is entitled READ AND PRAY.

Each page in a Read and Pray booklet contains a comment, reflection, and prayer on a brief passage of Scripture. In the **comment** the author, an expert in Scripture, distills the best of contemporary scholarship; in the **reflection** he prods the reader into pondering the relationship of the Scripture to daily life; in the **prayer** he invites the reader to respond to God's message.

The sequence, read and pray, is shorthand for the dynamic each book envisions. A fuller sequence would be: 1) pray for the Spirit's guidance; 2) read the Scripture passage assigned; 3) read the comment and reflection; 4) reflect on your own; 5) read the prayer; 6) pray on your own.

It is our hope that this series will be of benefit to daily and Sunday homilists, shared prayer groups, Bible study groups, and to all those who seek in Scripture spirit and life.

THE AUTHOR, a member of the Vincentian Community, Province of the West, holds a Licentiate in Scripture from the Pontifical Biblical Institute in Rome. He teaches Scripture at St. John's Seminary in Camarillo, California.

ROBERT J. KARRIS O.F.M.
Catholic Theological Union at Chicago

N.B. Unless otherwise noted, all Scripture quotations are based on the Revised Standard Version.

READ AND PRAY

Daily Bible Readings, with
Comments, Reflections, Prayers,
One Page a Day
For Three Months

GOSPEL OF ST. MARK

by

PHILIP VAN LINDEN, C.M.

FRANCISCAN HERALD PRESS
CHICAGO, ILLINOIS 60609

Read and Pray, No. 4: *Gospel of St. Mark* by Philip Van Linden, C.M. Copyright © 1976 by Franciscan Herald Press, 1434 West 51st Street, Chicago, Illinois 60609. Made in the United States of America.

Library of Congress Cataloging in Publication Data:

Van Linden, Philip.
   The Gospel of St. Mark.

   (Read and pray)
   1. Bible. N.T. Mark—Devotional literature. I. Title. II. Series.
BS2585.V28   242   76-46627
ISBN 0-8199-0630-1

NIHIL OBSTAT:
   Mark Hegener O.F.M.
   Censor

IMPRIMATUR:
   Msgr. Richard A. Rosemeyer, J.D.
   Vicar General, Archdiocese of Chicago

September 20, 1976

How to Use
Read and Pray

1. Before reading the Scripture passage indicated, make up your mind to give this time to prayerful reflection and communion with God.

2. Then read over the Scripture passage slowly, from first to last. Do not jump ahead. ONLY ONE PAGE A DAY.

3. Then read the "Comment" in READ AND PRAY for the day's selection, meditatively, sentence by sentence, giving each thought time to make its impression. Re-read the Scripture passage and "Comment" again if you find it necessary.

4. Now turn to God, to our Lord, to the Blessed Mother and in familiar terms speak to them about what you feel you must do, and will do, and would like to do as a result of your reflection. Use "Reflection" in READ AND PRAY to assist you in these meditative responses to your considerations and meditations on the Scripture passage.

5. In closing, offer the prayer at the bottom of the page or any other prayer that you think appropriate or which may come to your mind and heart spontaneously. Thank God!

COMMENT: Mark's first verse is actually the title and theme sentence of his whole gospel. The early Christian community in 70 A.D. was very discouraged as it faced suffering and persecution for the sake of its faith in Jesus. Mark wanted his fellow Christians to hear and to proclaim the "good news" (the meaning of the Greek word for "gospel") about Jesus, their Lord. Mark's descriptive names for Jesus are very significant. "Christ" for the early believer was more than Jesus' last name. It also meant "messiah-savior." Peter is the first person in the gospel to recognize Jesus as Messiah (8:29). Jesus will respond: "take up your cross and follow me" (8:34). The only other human being to call Jesus "the Son of God" is the Roman centurion at the foot of the cross (15:39). Thus, both descriptive names point to Jesus' way of saving man: the way of the cross.

REFLECTION: Jesus' saving victory over death and sin was "good news" to the first Christians. But his way of saving us, through suffering and death, was and still is difficult to understand. We join Mark's Christians in pondering: why we still suffer, as we try to live good Christian lives. Can't we expect an easier way than Jesus' way?

Father, make me open to your "good news" about your beloved son, as I begin to pray St. Mark's Gospel.

COMMENT: While the Gospels of Matthew and Luke begin with Jesus' birth, Mark has the prophets (Malachi 3:1 and Isaiah 40:3) and John the Baptizer prepare the way for the Lord's coming among his people as a mighty, full-grown man (vs. 2f. and 7f.) Although Mark devotes the first verses of his gospel to John's ministry of repentance and baptism by water (vs. 4f), it is clear that he has no interest in John except as the forerunner of the Messiah. Even the description of John's clothing and diet (v. 6) remind Mark's readers of the prophet Elijah, who came to his people "wearing a hairy garment with a leather girdle about his loins" (2 Kings 1:8). John was indeed the new Elijah, sent by God to prepare the way for the Lord. By verse 8, we are sure that the next person to come on the scene will be the Messiah himself (see 1:9).

REFLECTION: We join the followers of the Baptizer (and Mark) in looking forward to God's final coming, when the heavens will be opened and we will be at home with the Lord forever (cf. 2 Corinthians 5:1-10). Are we worthy to be in daily union with the risen Lord unless we turn away from sin, as John urges us? As Christians baptized with the Holy Spirit, do our lives point to Jesus and the Kingdom of God, as John's did?

A clean heart create for me, O God, and a steadfast spirit renew within me (Psalm 51:12).

COMMENT: The long-awaited Messiah of Israel and the Lord of Christians "came from Nazareth and was baptized by John in the Jordan" (v. 9). Mark has set the stage for Jesus' appearance (in vs. 2-8), and doesn't hesitate to have John baptize the Lord of Baptism with water (see Matthew, Luke, and John, who diminish John's role in Jesus' baptism). The Spirit descends upon Jesus from heaven like a dove (v. 10); and finally God himself confirms for Mark's readers in 70 A.D. that Jesus is his beloved and pleasing Son (vs. 10f.). This divine sonship is confirmed from heaven, even though the disciples and people of Jesus' own time didn't understand who he really was (see *Comment* on 1:1).

REFLECTION: Jesus was baptized by water and the Spirit, and he is clearly God's beloved son. We too are sons and daughters of God because of our baptism, when we first received the gift of the Spirit. Obviously, the gifts of sonship and Spirit within us can be neglected or ignored. So God urges us through Mark to reawaken our timid spirits, to use our gifts for others, and to recall our union with *the* son . . . "for God did not give us a spirit of timidity, but a spirit of power and love and self control" (2 Timothy 1:6f.).

Come Holy Spirit, fill the hearts of your faithful, and reenkindle in us the fire of your love.

COMMENT: It was in the desert wandering of forty days that God tested his people "by affliction and hunger, to find out whether or not it was their intention to keep his commandments" (Deut. 8:2ff.). The wilderness was also the place where God promised to speak to Israel's heart and to espouse a faithful people to himself forever (Hosea 2:16-25). In the light of such rich "desert" symbolism, the significance of Jesus' first act became clear to Mark and the early Christians: "The Messiah was led by the Spirit into the desert where he overcame Satan in a trial of strength; God provided assistance then (the angels); he will be with all his faithful ones, as they continue to choose God's way over the way of evil forces and inclinations."

REFLECTION: As members of a pilgrim people, we experience temptations to sin daily and recognize the power of evil inclinations within us. Each year at Easter time we renew our baptismal promises and renounce Satan and his works. Perhaps a daily renewal of such promises might make us more conscious of the fidelity we are called to, as God's children. Might we not also become more aware of God's fidelity toward us, and his powerful presence with us, as we journey toward him?

Jesus, you freed all your people from slavery to sin; protect me daily on my life's journey to you.

COMMENT: As the work of the "forerunner," John, finishes, the work of the "mightier one" begins (v. 14; cf. 1:7). In v. 15 Mark summarizes the gospel message that Jesus preached and *was*: "The time of waiting is over! God has sent his son to bring everything into harmony with his will! God's rule has begun! So turn away from sin to God, and place all your trust in his saving action!" In Jesus' day, this message would have exhilarated some of his Jewish brethren, full of messianic hopes for immediate deliverance from all forces of evil. Forty years later, Mark challenged his disheartened and persecuted Christians with the same message, in the light of the cross and resurrection: "Rely confidently on the God who brought our crucified Messiah to life; and realize that the power of his kingdom becomes evident in your loving lives of humble service."

REFLECTION: To believe in Jesus and in the gospel means to travel as Jesus did, humbly making God's kingdom present on earth through sacrificial love. Despite the daily suffering and frustration that come with Christian discipleship, the believing Christian will experience the uplifting power of God's kingdom!

Our Father, who art in heaven, hallowed be thy name; thy kingdom come, thy will be done!

COMMENT: Jesus calls four fishermen from their life work, and they follow him immediately. "The response to Jesus' call must be decisive, total, and immediate," says Mark. When the prophet Jeremiah was called (see Jeremiah 1:4-10), he hesitated because he was so young. The Lord reprimanded him: "Say not, 'I am too young.' To whomever I send you, you shall go; whatever I command you, you shall speak." When the prophet Elisha was called (see 1 Kings 19:19-21), he went to kiss his mother and father good-bye before following Elijah. When Jesus calls to discipleship, says Mark, you must leave your father "in the boat" and follow him immediately (v. 25; see also 10:28-30).

REFLECTION: Christian discipleship is radical. But does Jesus really ask us to leave our work and families to follow him today? What about the responsibilities we have to those who depend on us: to bring home the paycheck, to take care of the family, parents, etc.? God speaks radically through Mark and through his son, Jesus: "Follow me on my loving and suffering way. Carry one another's burdens. Care for your families with sacrificial devotion and responsibility. But don't forget that I am the one to whom you have given your whole self. Follow *me* as you serve me in your brothers!"

Here I am Lord; I come to do your will.

COMMENT: As Jesus begins his ministry of teaching and healing, it is very important for us to begin noting carefully what the evangelist Mark wants to communicate to his Christian believers. For example, as Mark's Jesus "teaches," we don't hear *what* he taught, but *how* he taught ("with authority," v. 22); and we see what the reaction of the people was to his teaching ("astonishment and amazement," vs. 22 & 27). The people in the synagogue recognized some authority in Jesus' new teaching and his power over the unclean spirit (v. 27); but the evil spirit alone recognized the true identity of Jesus (v. 24). For Mark and the early Christians, Jesus was indeed the powerful master over evil spirits (see also 3:11-12; 5:1-13; 7:25-30; and 9:14-29) and over death itself (16:6). But only four were truly devoted to him (1:16-20); the others are amazed, and his reputation "spread everywhere" (v. 28).

REFLECTION: As Jesus reveals himself to us today, cleansing our hearts and minds with his word and sacraments, do we recognize him for who he really is? As members of a society that is continually in need of purification, are we active participants in Jesus' ministry of healing and teaching? Or do we stand by, giving him mere verbal allegiance?

Holy one of God, cleanse me of all that is not holy within me. Purify me for your service.

COMMENT: There were many healers and exorcists at work in Jesus' time. They used special word-formulas and action-techniques to perform their cures. Jesus has just exorcised a demon by his word (1:25); and in this brief but touching story of his concern for Simon's mother-in-law, Mark shows that Jesus could also cure by a simple touch. (The words "and she served them," v. 31, dramatize the completeness of the cure.) In this story we continue to learn Mark's understanding of Jesus' healing ministry: he has supernatural power over the forces of evil. For in those days, illness was attributed to evil or sinful personal forces at work in sick people.

REFLECTION: Today many men and women lie sick in hospitals, in rest homes, and in rehabilitation centers, longing for the healing power of God. In the new *Rite of the Anointing of the Sick* the members of the sick person's family pray for the forgiveness of sins and for all those who care for the one suffering. The priest lays his hands on the sick person, before anointing him with the oil of the sick. By this sacramental action, and even in our brief, private visits with the sick, we are able to unite ourselves with our Lord's tender concern for the suffering members of his Body.

Lord, may your blessing come upon all who are sick and make them well again in body, mind, and soul.

COMMENT: Mark now describes a crowded scene at sundown: *"all* who were sick or possessed were there . . . the *whole city* was there . . . he healed *many,* afflicted with *various* diseases." Such an all-inclusive power could only be the power of God himself at work among his people (vs. 32-34a)! Our attention turns to the last half of v. 34 where Mark presents Jesus as being very reticent about disclosing "who he is." Elsewhere in Mark's Gospel the devils are told not to reveal his identity (3:12); those Jesus cured are forbidden to reveal it (1:44; 5:43; 7:36; 8:26); and even his closest friends are given strict orders not to tell anyone about him (8:30), at least not until after he has risen from the dead (9:9). Such commands to silence on Jesus' part have come to be known as "the Messianic Secret."

REFLECTION: Why did Jesus (and Mark) want to keep his messiahship a secret? Could it be because in Jesus' time, as today, there were various inadequate ideas of what a Messiah-hero was, and what he would do for us? We think of Jesus as the Messiah who will heal us and bring us peace; we might believe he will "put in their place" those who oppose goodness and truth. How many of our ideas about Jesus-Messiah include his own?

Jesus, Messiah, I know your secret; and I too choose to bring healing and peace by GIVING MY LIFE FOR OTHERS!

COMMENT: Jesus came to proclaim the coming of the Kingdom of God (v. 38; see 1:15). Peter and the others interrupted Jesus' prayer to tell him that all the people "were searching for him" (v. 36). But Mark says that Jesus knew they were searching him out for the wrong reason. They didn't want to hear his call to the kingdom by repentance and faith (1:15); they wanted the "miracle-worker" (1:21-34). So Jesus moves on, preaching throughout *all* of Galilee, casting out demons (v. 39). His mission has been misunderstood from the beginning! It is very significant that Mark has Jesus pray only three times in the entire gospel (1:35; 6:46; 17:32ff.). Each of these three times he prays alone. Each time he is in a stress situation. And each time his prayerful trust in his Father is contrasted with the misunderstanding and unbelief of the disciples.

REFLECTION: Mark asks us: "Are you searching for the Lord? When you find him alone, in your prayer, do you want to manipulate him into doing wonders for you? Or do you quietly unite your spirit with that of the misunderstood Messiah? Do you understand that you share his mission to proclaim the kingdom of God and the overwhelming love of God for all men . . . unto death on a cross?"

Jesus, enlighten me that I might humble myself, becoming obedient unto death, even death on a cross! (Philippians 2:5-11).

COMMENT: Even leprosy yields to the power of Jesus. In Jewish society, the Law could do nothing for the leper; it only protected the rest of the community against him, "the outcast." Mark here relates how the powerful Lord "was moved with pity" and cured the man with a word (v. 41). Jesus was also "moved with anger" (a more accurate rendering of "sternly charged" in v. 43) against the forces of disease, sin and Satan which the leprosy symbolized. Significantly, Jesus' attempt to conceal his identity (v. 44) is met by the disobedience of the leper who "began to talk freely about it" (v. 45). Jesus knew, implies Mark, that the people would hail him as a cure-all savior king. His true identity, that of "suffering servant" (see 10:45), was misunderstood from the first chapter of his life!

REFLECTION: God speaks to Christians today in these verses. "My beloved 20th century children: trust in my saving power. I understand your needs, and am moved with pity even today as I see you suffer. Come to me and experience the power of the resurrection in the pain and misunderstanding that goes with bearing the Christian cross you bear. Rejoice in my cleansing word so that you can live as my son did . . . healing others in need."

Thank you for healing me, Lord. And help me to understand what your contemporaries didn't: that you ultimately healed me from the cross.

COMMENT: Although Jesus had full respect for the Law of Moses (1:44), his growing reputation as miracle-worker brought him into many conflicts with the Pharisees about healing and Jewish theology. The cure of the paralytic causes the first of many such controversies (see the "chain" of five controversy stories that make up 2:1-3:6). Not only does Jesus have power over the man's paralysis (v. 11); in response to faith, "the Son of Man has authority on earth to forgive sins" (vs. 5 & 10). In Mark's day, the Christians' claim to forgiveness of sins through Jesus caused much offense to the Jews. Thus, the theological debate (in vs. 7-10) was emphasized to show that the claim was not blasphemous, because Jesus truly was the promised Son of Man! "Son of Man" was the Jewish title applied to the one sent from God through whom his kingdom would be established (see Daniel 7:13f.).

REFLECTION: Anyone would glorify God upon seeing such a miraculous cure (v. 12)! Wouldn't we also be amazed if a man whom we all knew claimed to be able to forgive sins? Yet Jesus does just that! Do we really know him as the one through whom our sins are forgiven. Do we rejoice when God grants us pardon and peace? Do we really believe him when he says to us: "My child, your sins are forgiven"?

"Happy is he whose fault is taken away, whose sin is covered. I confess my faults to the Lord, and you take away the guilt of my sin" (Psalm 32).

COMMENT: "The blasphemer claimed to forgive sins (2:7). Now he asks tax collectors to follow him (v. 14) and sinners to eat with him (v. 16)." Jesus becomes an even more controversial figure as he mixes with the outcasts of "respectable" Jewish society (v. 15ff.). The scribes of the Pharisees' party challenge the one who sits at table with people like the tax collector, Levi. (To have "table-fellowship" with another was regarded as a sign and pledge of real intimacy.) Even after Jesus' death and resurrection there would be "righteous" ones who would object seriously to sharing at the Eucharistic table with the lower, "sinful" ranks of society (see 1 Cor 11:17ff.). Mark's Christians needed to be reminded that "God chose the foolish, weak and despised of the world" (see 1 Cor 1:26-29). Jesus had not come for the righteous!

REFLECTION: What has happened to Christianity that has caused sinners and outcasts to feel that they "don't belong"? Why do people falsely think that the Church is for the righteous and "respectable" members of society? Are we willing to admit our own desperate need for Jesus, the physician? Do our hearts beat as Jesus' heart, which searched out and shared its love with those "on the fringes"?

Jesus, thank you for calling me, a sinner. Heal me. Make my heart like yours, as I join you and all your people at the Eucharistic table.

COMMENT: The third conflict story also has to do with eating (2:16) — and fasting. Some pious Jews object that Jesus' disciples have not joined them in observing a fast, which they might have been expected to do if they were really concerned for the kingdom of God (v. 18). Jesus explains why his disciples don't fast while the bridegroom is still with them (v. 19). Later, after Jesus' death, the Christian community once again began to fast regularly, but on days other than traditional Jewish fast days. Verse 20 and the parables that follow thus show that the Christian church had found it necessary to express its religious life through practices different from the ancient forms of Judaism (vs. 20-22).

REFLECTION: People don't fast as much as they did centuries or decades ago. But there is still a call to fasting that is proper to Christians, which finds its explanation in the mystery of Jesus' cross. The bridegroom has been taken from us and waits for us "to fill up what is lacking in the sufferings of Christ for the sake of his body, the Church" (Colossians 1:24; NAB). To deny ourselves in order to unite ourselves with Jesus and with the hungry and suffering members of the body is a noble, human, Christian act of love.

Jesus, my beloved, I choose to bear my part of the burden, as we wait for the fullness you bring.

COMMENT: Jesus' disciples seem to disregard all the prescriptions of the Law; they even "pluck ears of grain on the Sabbath" (vs. 23f.). In normal circumstances the Law allowed hungry travellers to help themselves in this way (Deut 23:25), but never on the Sabbath (Exodus 34:21). This causes the fourth conflict between Jesus and the Pharisees. Jesus meets the objection as a good rabbi would. "Look at the model of piety, King David. He frequently transgressed the Law because the Law was for man's good; and in exceptional circumstances the Law had to be subordinated to human needs" (vs. 25ff. refer back to 1 Samuel 21:1-6). In the last verse, the Son of Man (see *Comment* on 2:1-12) expresses the conviction that he is Lord of *all* that belongs to man, including the Sabbath. The controversy over the Sabbath is thus broadened to a general principle: the Son of Man and his Christian followers don't interpret the Law by the letter, but live according to its spirit.

REFLECTION: Today's developmental psychology suggests that we clarify our own values and help others clarify theirs. This approach is meant to move us away from an immature attitude towards life and "law": "you'll do it because I said so . . . I'm doing it because they said so."

Lord, as your maturing disciple, I want to fulfill the whole Law "by loving my neighbor as myself" (Galatians 5:14 and 6:2).

COMMENT: The controversies over theology and the Law (begun in 2:1) reach a peak after this cure in the synagogue on a Sabbath day. No longer do the pious ones argue with Jesus' ways (see 2:7ff., 16, 18, and 24). They remain silent in face of his challenge: "Is it lawful to do good on the Sabbath?" (vs. 4f.). But after the man's hand is cured by Jesus' word (v. 5), the Pharisees plotted how to destroy Jesus (v. 6). The plot thickens, only to reach its climax when Jesus' own arms are stretched out on the cross (15:24ff.). Thus all these early conflicts point to certain people's inability, or refusal, to see that Jesus is God's own son . . . even in Mark's day. No doubt this is why Mark records Jesus' anger and grief at the Pharisees' hardened hearts (v. 5; see Matt 12:13 and Luke 6:10, where such emotions are not mentioned).

REFLECTION: Many controversies rage today over religious values, practice and authority. The conflicts are as great within Christianity as they are between Christians and those of other faiths. We are a "withered people" when we refuse to go to the person whose anger might just shake us out of our petty self-concerns. Christians are meant to bring others together, not to divide further.

Lord, thank you for healing me. Teach me to stretch out my hands in healing reconciliation.

COMMENT: After a series of theological conflicts with Jesus (2:1-3:6), the Pharisees plotted to destroy him (3:6). Mark next contrasts the mounting hostility of the religious leaders of Jesus' time with the crowds of ordinary folk who sought him for his healing touch (vs. 7-10). In an even more striking contrast with the leaders, the unclean spirits recognize him as "the Son of God" that he was (v. 11)! (At the end of this chapter Mark will report the scribes' accusation that Jesus himself was possessed by the devil, in 3:22!) In this way Mark explains why the people of God needed new leaders with hearts and minds open to the Lord. (Cf. the following section in which Jesus appoints the twelve as his co-workers.) The fact that Jesus orders the unclean spirits "not to make him known" (v. 12) is in line with Mark's "messianic secret" (cf. 1:32-34).

REFLECTION: Today, God asks us through Mark: "In this hectic world of ours, are you and your actions misunderstood, even by your loved ones?" Even when we are trying our very best to be good Christians, we often must respond "yes." In such trying moments, do we realize how closely related we are to the misunderstood Lord? Do we pause and pray, with him:

Companion and neighbor you have taken away from me; but I, O Lord, cry out to you; with my morning prayer I wait upon you (from Psalm 88).

COMMENT: In 1:16-20 St. Mark described Jesus' call to discipleship. Here Jesus calls the twelve to the mountain (v. 13) where he officially appoints them "to be with him" and "to be sent out to preach and to cast out demons" (v. 14). He also names the twelve (vs. 16-19). Later, in 6:7-13, Jesus will call the twelve together again; and this time he will actually "send them out" to take an active part in his ministry. By keeping the "mission" of the twelve until later in his gospel (compare Matt 10:2-5), Mark shows that the disciples must first "be with" the Lord before they are "sent out." (They need to *hear* him, in the parables of ch. 4; they also need to *see* more of his healing ministry, in 4:35-6:6. Then they will be ready. Or will they?)

REFLECTION: We are called to be apostles. We are "sent out" (the meaning of the Greek word "apostle") to spread the good news of Jesus that we have heard and experienced. Eager to be active in the apostolate of Christian service, we are urged by God through St. Mark: "I call you by name, to be my apostles. But you cannot give what you haven't got. So be with me. Listen, watch, and learn from me. Then you will have much to give to those to whom I send you."

Jesus, my Teacher, feed me with your word and prepare your weak apostle for your work among your people.

COMMENT: Many people crowd around Jesus, the healer-exorcist (v. 20; see 3:9-11). His friends think he is "beside himself" (v. 21). The scribes think he is possessed by the devil (vs. 22-27 & 30). Even his mother and brethren don't understand him! (Note the significant contrast between his family "outside" and the crowd "sitting about him" in vs. 31ff.) Only those who do the will of God can really know him as "brother" and Lord (v. 35)! In two parables, Mark's Jesus shows how absurd it is to think that he does good things by an evil power (vs. 24-26); in fact, he is the "mightier" one who overcame the devil in the desert (v. 27; cf. 1:12f.). The misunderstood Messiah points out that *the* unforgiveable sin belongs to his accusers, who refuse to accept the power of God (the Holy Spirit) at work in him (vs. 28-30).

REFLECTION: While Jesus lived among us, very few people interpreted his power and purpose correctly. We often wonder why our omnipotent God acts like he does in our complicated lives. He responds in these verses by inviting us to "come inside and sit around him." He asks us to discern with him his Father's will for us and to experience his power in living single-hearted lives of love.

Happy are they who observe the decrees of the Lord, who seek him with all their heart (Psalm 119).

COMMENT: As Jesus begins "to teach beside the sea" (v. 1), we are brought into the familiar, first-century world of parables. Teaching in parables was a common way that Jesus and his contemporaries challenged their listeners to understand something new and more profound in their familiar, daily experiences. So "listen carefully" to the parable about "a sower who went out to sow" (v. 3). And "let him who has ears to hear, understand the deeper meaning in this simple story!" (v. 9). Mark and his Church of the 70's would apply the parable in a particular way (Mark 4:13-20); i.e., the seed is Jesus' all-powerful word that would produce a great harvest, in spite of the opposition and indifference it was receiving in the world of the early Church.

REFLECTION: How do we respond in our daily lives to Jesus' invitation to hear his first parable? As a married person, how do I respond to God's gift of marriage and my family? As a sister, seminarian, priest or brother, how do I respond to the gift of my vocation? And do we have the hope that God's gifts and word to us will produce much fruit, in spite of the daily difficulties we face?

My Jesus, I accept your challenge to see you at work in my familiar, daily life. Help me respond in hope to whatever you offer me!

COMMENT: This strange and harsh sounding section of Mark's Gospel has sometimes been interpreted as meaning that Jesus used parables to hide his teaching from the crowds. This is not the meaning of the evangelist Mark. Jesus' parables were meant to stimulate thought and bring all people closer to God's kingdom. However, the early Church knew clearly that Jesus' teaching *had* been rejected in his lifetime. Why hadn't people believed in him? Why, instead, had they put him to death? In this passage Mark explains that Jesus knew *some* would understand him and believe in him ("you disciples" in v. 11). Jesus *didn't want* Isaiah's prophecy to come true (Isa 6:9-10, quoted by Mark in v. 12), but he knew that some would reject Jesus' invitation to faith . . . as indeed, some did!

REFLECTION: All sincere Christians want to be "on the inside," intimately involved with Jesus, our Lord and Teacher. We have a lifetime to understand the secrets of God's kingdom and the Christian way of life, and we have God's Word and his Church to guide us. But will we be open to such guidance? Or will we see without perceiving and hear without understanding, and thus remain "outside"?

Here I am, Lord. Be with me and heal my blindness. Help my heart understand your ways so that I can turn fully to you!

COMMENT: At the end of Mark's chapter of Jesus' parables, we learn that the Lord "explained everything to his own disciples privately" (4:34). In vs. 14-20 we see how Mark has inserted an explanation of the parable of the sower for his own Christians in 70 A.D.! As Mark's community listened carefully, they could hear various elements of Jesus' parable being applied to their own circumstances. At first, the sower's seed is *God's word* (v. 14); but then the seeds become the *different kinds of people* who receive the word (vs. 15ff.). Each detail of the parable now takes on a special meaning. For example, the seed on thorny ground becomes the dangerous desire for riches which lure some persons away from the Word of God (vs. 18f.). It becomes clear that Mark is applying Jesus' parable to his own community, whose faith is being challenged by the threats of persecution (the rocky ground in vs. 16f.). In these circumstances, he calls for the acceptance of Jesus' word and the fruitful practice of the Christian faith (v. 20).

REFLECTION: We join Mark's community by questioning ourselves as Mark urges. What sort of "ground" am I? Do indifference, suffering, or wealth lure me from the faith of Jesus? Am I bearing the sort of fruit that the Lord expects of me?

Bless the Lord, O my soul; and all my being, bless his holy name. Forget not all his benefits! (Psalm 103)

COMMENT: After the parable of the sower and its application (vs. 1-20), Mark combines five or six separate sayings of Jesus into two little parables (vs. 21-23 and 24-25). The first parable about the lamp (v. 21) suggests that Jesus' teaching must come to full light, even though some of its depths might not immediately be understood (v. 22). Mark's disciples are thus call in the 70's to hear Jesus' message in all its depths, so that they can explain it properly to others in their day (v. 23).

REFLECTION: We pause after these few short verses to ask ourselves if we are truly growing in our personal knowledge of Jesus. Parish adult education programs and continuing education efforts for priests and sisters are becoming more and more a part of the Church's life. Do we participate in them willingly? Do we support and encourage those responsible for organizing such efforts? Do we admit that we still have much to learn about Jesus' church and our response to him? Moreover, as we learn, are we becoming more willing to share our own experience of Jesus and our faith with others?

Lord, I thank you for helping me know you more deeply and more personally. May I be the light that draws others to you.

COMMENT: This parabolic saying about "what you give is what you get" (vs. 24-25) is closely connected with the preceding parable about the lamp (vs. 21-23). The disciples of Mark's day must continuously grow in their understanding of Jesus' life and its meaning, or they will lose what they think they possess (v. 24). Mark's Christians will grow in their understanding and imitation of Jesus, or else their empty lives and words will prove that they *never did commit themselves* to Jesus and his way (v. 25).

REFLECTION: "Take heed what you hear, my brothers and sisters of the twentieth century. You have been given so much over the centuries, since the time when I first wrote this gospel. The living Word of God has spoken to the Church throughout the ages and is as relevant to your lives today as it was in my day. Is the world around you (in your parish and neighborhood) more aware of the true meaning of Jesus' life and message of loving concern because of your example?" So speaks Mark to us today, as we hear these two simple verses.

St. Mark, I thank you for challenging me to be a living witness to the gospel which you so forcefully preached to your first parishioners, and which I hear this day!

COMMENT: By this parable about the kingdom of God and the sleeping farmer, Mark's Jesus emphasizes the fact that it is God and not man who ultimately brings about the establishment of God's reign. Just as a seed grows of its own accord, so the kingdom of God has its own inner power that is beyond man's control (vs. 26f.). "So be trusting and patient now," says Mark to his first Christians, eager to see God's rule fully established in their own day, "for God will finish his work when it is time" (v. 29).

REFLECTION: It is legitimate to question God's ways in our world and in our lives, especially when so much seems to go wrong so often. We try to be a light to the world and we are rejected. We end up by asking "does it really pay to live a loving Christian life?" Through Mark God calls us to be patient and trusting with *his* plans for his kingdom. In the context of Mark's entire gospel, we know that this does not mean that our part in the kingdom is a passive one. The parable merely reminds us that ultimately it is *his* work we do, not our own . . . a reminder that many of us need when our faith and hope are constantly shaken.

Our Father, thy kingdom come, thy will be done!

COMMENT: "The kingdom of God is like the smallest of seeds that quickly grows to become the greatest of all shrubs." This last parable in ch. 4 is meant to encourage the primitive church in its missionary activity, often stifled by persecution and fear of persecution. "No matter how insignificant our numbers and 'success' might seem to be now," Mark says to his community in the 70's, "the kingdom of God will one day bring all people within its powerful and loving grasp. Be encouraged by Jesus' example of the tiny mustard seed that grows to be so large!"

REFLECTION: "If God's kingdom really began to be established in Jesus, why has so little happened over twenty centuries? Why does evil continue to be so prevalent today? Why do I still find myself stumbling in sin and weakness, failing to live up to Jesus' demands of discipleship?" Is not God encouraging us by this parable of the mustard seed to seek the answers to our questions in the heart of his church? Might we not profit by a quiet and trusting admission of how many great things he has done with his humble handmaidens and servants? Let's join in Mary's prayer, which is the Church's prayer today:

My soul magnifies the Lord, for he has regarded the lowliness of his handmaid. He who is mighty has truly done great things for me and holy is his name (Lk 1:47ff.).

READING   Mark 4:33-34

COMMENT: After relating Jesus' parables about the kingdom, Mark concludes with this summary statement: "Many people had listened to Jesus, and some were able to grasp something of what he had shared with them (v. 33). But to his disciples he privately explained everything" (v. 34). With such private instruction and tutoring, one would presume that the disciples were almost completely in union with their Lord, understanding his message and trusting in him without question. Mark allows his readers to presume this, but only for a moment. For we next find Jesus and his disciples out at sea (vs. 35-41), where the disciples show the total lack of their understanding and faith!

REFLECTION: When we ponder Mark's summary statement that rounds off the parables and leads into the passage about the storm on the sea, we really must wonder what God is trying to say to us today. Although we pride ourselves on having great insights into Christianity, and can even explain much of the church's teaching to others, how deeply are we in touch with our teacher and Lord, Jesus? How does our knowledge of the faith stand up in stormy waters, when real life and real conflicts crush in upon us?

St. Mark, I ask you to intercede with my Father to help me live my faith. I so want to live the gospel today, where God has put me!

COMMENT: After disclosing the secrets of the kingdom to his disciples (4:34), Jesus exhibits his power over nature, as he quiets the violent storm with a word: "Peace! Be still!" (v. 39). Besides manifesting the divine ability to control the sea and storms (see Exodus 15:8; Psalms 93:3f. and 106:8f.; Isa 51:9f.), Jesus also manifests a perfect trust in the protective power of God, sleeping peacefully while the disciples are afraid of perishing (v. 38). The disciples and the early Church had to be asked: "Why are you afraid? Have you no faith?" (v. 40). Just as God led his people through the Red Sea, he will also protect the Ark of his church when it is buffeted by waves of persecution and suffering. Believe in Jesus, even when he seems to be asleep or far removed from your plight.

REFLECTION: It is easy to read this passage and conclude by saying: "Those poor, blind disciples! Didn't they realize the Son of God was with them and wouldn't let them die at sea?" Even though they exhibited fear and no faith, they at least approached him. How often do we turn to him in our troubles *only after* we have tried "everything else"?

"Awake! Why are you asleep, O Lord? Arise, help us! Redeem us for your kindness' sake" (Psalm 44).

COMMENT: Who can this Jesus be, that even ferocious evil spirits come out of a possessed man at his command? After the unusually vivid descriptions of the possessed man's destructive strength and self-mutiliation (vs. 2-5), Jesus' dialogue with him and his cure (vs. 6-13) are convincing signs that Jesus truly is the Son of the most high God, deserving of worship (vs. 5f.). It is also very significant that this is the first time that Mark places Jesus in non-Jewish territory (v. 1; see also vs. 11-14: Jews were forbidden even to keep swine). This miracle story, along with the cure of the Syrophoenician's daughter in 7:24-30, set the stage for the future spread of Christianity to the Gentiles. Mark's gentile Christians can thus look back to this incident and see that Jesus had indeed intended his saving word to be proclaimed to them, as Mark was now doing (vs. 19-20).

REFLECTION: "Let us stay with you, for you have done such wonderful things for us!" "No, my sons and daughters. Go to your homes and to your friends. There, where you live and work, proclaim what I have done for you. Make my healing power present among them by your loving witness to the gospel!"

"To you we owe our hymn of praise, O God; you still the roaring of the seas and the tumult of the peoples" (Psalm 65).

COMMENT: Two miracle stories are joined together by Mark in a special way. They do not follow one another, but are "dove-tailed" together: the first story begins, the second is related in full, and the first one is completed. This is not only for dramatic effect. Mark saw similarities in the two stories that merited such intimate connection: both are healing miracles involving women, both involve Jesus' presence among the crowds. Most importantly, Mark has brought out one powerful message in the combination of the similar stories: faith in Jesus (vs. 34 and 36), even in impossible situations, brings healing and life; fear (vs. 33 and 36) is out of place in one's relationship with him. The human side of Jesus is emphasized in v. 30 where he doesn't know who touched him, in v. 34 when he calls the woman "daughter," and in v. 43 when he reminds the parents to feed the girl.

REFLECTION: What is the impossible situation you find yourself in at this stage of your life? A sickness that has plagued you for years? The impending loss of a loved one? Fear and despair are not the answers. Nor is a blind faith that has no person as its object. Invite the powerful Jesus, who is also so tenderly human, to come to your home. Trust the one who cures and gives life.

Increase my faith in you. Touch my life with your healing, Lord, and bless me with your life-giving Spirit. Free me from fear.

COMMENT: In 70 A.D., Mark's gentile Christians did not understand how the gospel of Jesus could have been rejected by the Jews, his own people. Jesus' saying (in v. 4) reminds them that other prophets of God had been rejected by their own people (e.g., Jeremiah; see Jer 18:18-23 and 20:7-18). The situation was no different with Jesus, who had just given three miraculous signs of his true identity (4:35-5:43). His people marveled at his works (v. 2); but their false ideas of an all-glorious Messiah hardly coincided with the (crucified) one whose mother and relatives they all knew (v. 3). Because they were scandalized at the "home-town boy" and his works (v. 4), "he could do no mighty works there" (v. 5; contrast Matt 13:58: he "could not do *many* mighty works there").

REFLECTION: The mention of Jesus' "brothers and sisters" (v. 3) often disconcerts those who don't realize that Mark was writing before the Church had developed its belief in Mary's perpetual virginity. Such a preoccupation with Jesus' family can distract us from what is central to Mark's message here: will you, who call Jesus your brother and Lord, also refuse to believe in him (v. 6)?

Jesus, Son of Mary and my Brother, keep me faithful to you.

COMMENT: A third time Jesus "calls" his special disciples to himself (v. 7; see 1:18 and 3:13). Now he sends them out (the Greek word for "apostle" means "one sent out"). They are sent to call others away from sin, to heal them from sickness, and to cast out demons (vs. 7 & 12f.). The radical call "Follow me!" (see 1:17) now becomes very specific: the followers are asked to share in his own ministry, travelling without special clothes, bread or money; they shall stay where hospitality is offered; and they shall perform a symbolic action when they are rejected (vs. 8-11; "shaking off the dust from their shoes" is a sign of God's rejection of those who refuse to accept his disciples). The language of these directives indicates that Jesus and the early Church saw the necessity of moving quickly and of depending totally on God's providence in their mission. "Repent and believe; the kingdom of God is at hand" (1:15).

REFLECTION: On our mission of Christian reconciliation and healing, we know that the risen Lord is with us. As we continue to build up the Church by our activity, are we really conscious of our dependence on our Lord? That it is by his authority that we act? Do we pause in the midst of our feeble efforts in order to strip ourselves of all unnecessary "baggage"?

Into your hands, O Lord, I commend my spirit!

COMMENT: The popular report of the death of John the Baptist is sometimes referred to as the only story in the Gospel that is not a story about Jesus. However, Mark refers to John in this section here, not only to tell of the heroic death of a prophet of truth. Nor is the story included here merely because Mark is forced to tell of the Baptist's fate. A careful reading shows how John, who prepared Jesus' way at the beginning of his ministry (1:2-11), also prepares for its ending. For Jesus also will be raised up (v. 14). The chief priests will also want to kill Jesus, but hesitate because of the people's reaction to him (vs. 19f.). And wouldn't Pilate also see Jesus as a man without guilt (v. 20)? Indeed, the fate of John prefigures the fate of Jesus. John was Jesus' forerunner, unto death!

REFLECTION: Herod confused the upright and holy John, whom he had killed, with the popular Jesus, who would also be killed — and be raised up. Do people in our society confuse us with the one we proclaim as Lord? Are we worthy of the name "Christian"? Have we prepared the way for his coming into the hearts of others? Will we die because of love and truth, as John and Jesus?

Lord Jesus, instill in me the courage of John. Let others see your loving sacrifice when they see me.

COMMENT: After the account of the forerunner's death (vs. 14-29), Mark brings his readers back to see how the apostles have carried out the mission Jesus had given them (vs. 7-13). The disciples need a rest (v. 31) as much as the crowds need a shepherd to teach them (v. 34; Jesus is like the good shepherd of Ezechiel 34:5ff.). But the shepherd also feeds his flock. The miracle of the loaves was most significant to the members of the early Church. It reminded them of God's greatest act of salvation in the *past*, when he fed his starving people in the desert with manna (Exodus 16 and Numbers 11). As Jesus, "the host," sees that his "guests" are satisfied (vs. 39-44), the Christian hope for the *future* messianic banquet is nourished. All comes together in the *present* experience of the early Church: for the actions of Jesus (v. 41) are exactly the same as those of the Last Supper (14:22) and their Eucharist!

REFLECTION: Weary and hungry, we come to the Lord for rest and food. In his nourishing word "he teaches us how he always loved his own in the world" (Euch. Prayer IV). "We hope to enjoy forever the vision of his glory," as we are "nourished by his body and blood. Thus we become one body, one Spirit, in Christ" (Euch. Prayer III).

It is right to give thanks and praise to you, O Lord, our God!

COMMENT: To members of the early Church, with the death and resurrection events behind them, the meaning of Jesus' miracles became clearer. Only God has mastery over the sea: therefore, Jesus is the Son of God (see parallel in Mt 14:22ff., especially v. 33). However, Mark realized that many members of his "informed" community in 70 A.D. were almost as blind and lacking in understanding about Jesus' mission as the first disciples were (vs. 51f.). So Mark deliberately combines this nature miracle with the previous story of the loaves (v. 45 & v. 52 show this). "In your distress and hunger, I come to you (v. 48). Take heart, it is I; have no fear (v. 50). Call out to me in faith, not in terror (v. 49). See me as the source of all calm and life!"

REFLECTION: God speaks dramatically to us through Mark: "Misunderstanding, fright and astonishment are all passive attitudes that must be put aside in your relationship with my Son. 'Crying out' might be your first act of real participation in Christianity. But then "take heart," and take him seriously. See that he truly does have the power to rescue you, no matter how desperate your situation. And he will!"

"He reached out from on high and grasped me; he drew me out of the deep waters. He rescued me, because he loves me" (Psalm 18).

COMMENT: This summary of Jesus' activity is Mark's way of emphasizing the healing power of Jesus (v. 56). It also contrasts the enthusiastic response of those who recognized Jesus in faith (vs. 54ff.) with the attitude of the Jewish religious leaders who refused to see and be healed and are featured in the conflicts in ch. 7, which follow immediately. Mark thus encourages his Christian readers to focus their faith on the one who has just said to them: "Take heart, it is I; have no fear" (6:50).

REFLECTION: Today many people are seeking Jesus as the source of wholeness and peace. Those who seek his healing are not only the sick, but also those who are disillusioned with the emptiness they find elsewhere. In our own search for him, we are called to express our faith concretely to others who seek him. The vivid language God uses here through St. Mark is an invitation to us to give others more than Jesus' name . . . it is our turn to touch and care for his people in his stead.

Jesus, my healing Lord and source of peace, use me to touch others with your loving care.

COMMENT: Although Jesus' healing ministry was powerful and successful (as Mark just reported at the end of ch. 6), Mark does not let his Christian readers forget that this ministry would end in the "failure" of the cross because of man's pride and blindness. Thus he begins ch. 7 with a series of Jesus' teachings that emphasized the conflict Jesus had with the Pharisees and scribes. "Such preoccupations with ritual washing practices are clearly superficial and hypocritical" says Mark's Jesus (vs. 3f.). "They hardly compare with what Isaiah knew God wanted from his people, namely, adherence to God's commands" (vs. 6-8). The other example of such false piety which Mark inserts here (vs. 9-13) brings out the same message. However, this example must reflect some peculiar and isolated circumstance in Jesus' or Mark's time, because no Jewish rabbi would condone such a blatant failure of filial duty toward one's parents.

REFLECTION: Unwittingly, the modern day Christian can read these verses with eyes and heart more closed and prejudiced than Mark's Pharisees! Instead of condemning them, Mark asks us *to ask ourselves*: Do *our* social customs exclude some of our neighbors from our "circle"? Do *we* worship on Sunday with our lips only, or do we live what we say?

Lord, you have made me and know my heart. Cleanse me of all prejudice and narrowness so that I might worship you with a pure intention!

COMMENT: Jesus' prophetic and sweeping statement in v. 15 seems to wipe out all the Jewish food laws found in the book of Leviticus. Jesus is presented here as having a much freer attitude toward the scriptural commands than the scribes, who insisted on food laws *because* they were commanded in the scriptures. But when Mark's Jesus explains the "parable" to his disciples (v. 17ff.), he declares foods clean *because* "it is not what a man eats that defiles him, but what he does" (vs. 18-20)! And so follows a list of real evils that his disciples should be concerned about avoiding (vs. 21f.). "This is what it means to take the law of God seriously," implies Mark's Jesus.

REFLECTION: "Let the man among you who has no sin be the first to cast a stone . . ." (John 8:7). While not many of our contemporaries are overly concerned with religious food laws, we can't forget our recent Catholic preoccupation with meat on Friday. The world is full of sinners, but do *we* take God's law seriously? Might we not profit from an honest self-evaluation in the light of vs. 21-22?

"Happy the man who delights in the law of the Lord and meditates on his law day and night" (Psalm 1).

COMMENT: Mark's Jesus turns from his harsh words with the Pharisees to perform a miracle for a non-Jewish woman (by religion she is "Greek," and by descent she is "Syrophoenician," v. 26). He cures her possessed daughter by a word, without even going to see her (vs. 29f.). But what is all-important is the surprising dialogue that precedes the miracle (vs. 27-29a). The Gentile shows her faith in the Lord by "falling at his feet" (v. 26). Then Jesus surprises her (and Mark's readers) by refusing to give to Gentiles (the dogs) what rightfully belongs to the Jews (the children), in v. 27. The lady agrees with Jesus, but persists and wins him over (v. 28). The exception is made and the little Gentile girl is healed (v. 29).

REFLECTION: After the resurrection, the early Church gradually came to understand that God truly meant to share his life-giving spirit and bread with all people, whatever their nationality. As well as imitating the woman's faith and persistence, we might well reflect on our attitudes toward God's special children, the Jews. Do we reach out to our Jewish brethren as Jesus reached out to the non-Jew? Or are we modern-day, prejudiced hypocrites (see Mark 7:6f.), refusing to open our hearts to those first called (see Exodus 19:3ff.)?

Cleanse me of all sin and prejudice, for you are Lord of all peoples!

COMMENT: Mark is the only evangelist who gives this detailed account of the cure of the deaf-mute. If you read it carefully in connection with another miracle story found only in Mark (the blind man in 8:22-26), you will notice how closely the two accounts parallel one another: the people first bring the sick person to Jesus and beg Jesus to touch him; Jesus then takes the sick one off by himself, touches him, applies spittle, speaks to him, and the cure is effected. In both cases Jesus says: "Tell no one." The two stories taken together show that (for Mark) Jesus is the Messiah that Isaiah promised long ago (Isa 35:5-6 reads: "then will the eyes of the blind be opened, the ears of the deaf be cured . . ."). The powerful Messiah and the intercessor with God the Father (v. 34) *is truly here*; but a deeper understanding and response is asked of Christians than "astonishment" (v. 37).

REFLECTION: The Lord works miracles in the lives of people today as he did in 30 A.D.: a death-bed conversion, the return home of an embittered child, the cure of one diseased beyond hope and doctors' help. Besides thanking the Lord and being astonished at his work in our lives, do we deepen our commitment to know him as he is, the Messiah who calls us to follow him all the way, where he goes (see 8:34ff.)?

Lord, you have done everything well. I will follow you!

COMMENT: In the second feeding of the multitude, Jesus takes the initiative, this time with a "heart moved with pity for the crowd" (vs. 1-3; NAB). Mark obviously has the Christian Eucharist in mind: "Jesus gives bread, superabundantly. He gives life. Eat and be satisfied." The two accounts of the miraculous feeding (chs. 6 and 8) seem to be two versions of one event. The vocabulary and actions in each are similar. Also, the question in v. 4 is out of place if the feeding in ch. 6 had just taken place. This second version is a later, more developed recount of the one event, aimed at a Christian community no longer made up of many Jewish converts. The seven loaves and seven baskets of leftovers move us away from the "Jewish" symbolism of five loaves (five books of Law) and twelve baskets (the twelve tribes of Israel?) of ch. 6. The bread of life is not only for the Jewish Christian. It is for all!

REFLECTION: Each Sunday, Catholic Christians all over the world gather together for the breaking of the bread. Through our active participation in Christ's act we are called to communion with the source of all life. We come hungry and long to be filled. Do we truly unite with him who gave up his life to give us life?

Lord, I am hungry for the living bread you are. I long for total union with you.

COMMENT: Mark interrupts his "chain" of miracle stories with another reminder of the Pharisees' continuing refusal to see God at work in Jesus (see also 7:1-23). Jesus' own refusal to give any further sign to "this generation" (v. 12; compare with Matt 12:38-42 & 16:1-4, where the sign of the resurrection *is* promised) recalls God's previous frustrations with his people in the desert: "Of all the man who have seen my glory and the signs I have worked in Egypt and in the desert, and who nevertheless have failed to heed my voice, not one shall see the land which I have promised on oath to their fathers" (Numbers 14:22f.). Mark's Jesus thus leads his readers into the long section of his gospel that deals with "the opening of the eyes of the blind disciples" (8:22-10:52). Will Mark's Christians see and accept Jesus, or will they also remain blind (see 4:10-13)?

REFLECTION: It is all too easy for us to look on the Pharisees of Jesus' time and the Hebrews in the desert with a self-righteous and judgmental attitude. In this way we join them in their blindness. God calls us to express our faith-vision by being signs of his love today. Does our life-style before and after the Eucharist prove we are faithful Christians? (See 8:1-10 and 8:14-21.)

Jesus, make me a sign of your love in the world this day.

COMMENT: Who is Jesus? He is the one who has multiplied a few loaves of bread for thousands of people (6:30ff. and 8:1ff.). He is the one who saves from death at sea (6:45ff.). He is the one who heals the sick (6:53ff.; 7:24ff.; 7:31ff.). He is the one who argues victoriously with the hostile experts of the Law (7:1ff. and 8:11ff.), who are like bad leaven (8:15). Who is Jesus? "Are your hearts still so hardened that you don't understand that I am the one loaf?" (v. 14). In Mark's day, in the midst of persecution of the Christians for their faith in Jesus, he challenges them: "Will unwillingness and fear keep you from seeing and accepting the hidden, yet ever-present Jesus, who is our life-giving bread?" What a perfect introduction to the cure of the blind man!

REFLECTION: In no other passage in the gospel does God prod us with more penetrating questions than here in ch. 8. How long will we, who claim to be Christians, fail to perceive who he really is? In our troubles, sometimes petty and sometimes momentuous, we are called to understand that he is with us. Do we understand yet, in the twentieth century? Or are we as blind as the disciples in the boat with Jesus? In our pursuit of the truth, do we seek him who is truth?

Jesus, soften and enlarge my hardened and petty heart. Open up my eyes and ears to see and to hear you.

COMMENT: It has already been mentioned that this particular cure of the blind man is only found in Mark's Gospel and is meant to bring out Jesus' identity as the Messiah promised by Isaiah (see *Comment* on 7:31-37). Since this cure immediately precedes the "key" section of Mark's Gospel, in which Jesus first calls for the total commitment of his disciples to his way of the cross (8:27-9:1), it becomes clear that the blind man is more than an historical figure. He personifies all of Jesus' disciples, in Jesus' time, in Mark's time, and always! Being cured from blindness, whether physical or spiritual blindness, takes time. It is a gradual process. Mark asks: "Do you really see who Jesus is? Do you really see the difference between Jesus' way and the views of the worldly-wise Pharisees? Do you see all clearly? Read on!" (See 8:27-9:1.)

REFLECTION: Today, it is a fact that people of all ages are looking for someone to believe in and to follow. We seek a powerful leader, but also one who will reach out and touch us personally. Are we humble enough to see that such a leader is here? Do we admit that he has cured us "in stages" and has led us to enough Christian maturity so that we can now respond as he wants us to respond?

Jesus, you have touched me and helped me see more clearly who you are and what Christianity is. Gratefully, I rededicate myself to you this day.

COMMENT: In this section Mark reflects further on the blindness of those closest to Jesus. Peter and the disciples regarded Jesus as a prophet or a Messiah. They watched him as if he were a spectacular actor on a stage, curing all the sick and doing all things well (chs. 1-8). Mark, who knows that Jesus *must suffer* (v. 31) before the drama can come to an end, reflects on the meaning of Jesus' life and question: "Who do *you* say that I am?" (v. 29). He knows that Peter's answer (v. 29) is true only if the title "the Christ" is understood in the sense of Jesus' favorite self-designation, the "Son of Man." The "Son of Man" title implied the necessity of Jesus' suffering and death. Such was God's plan for man's redemption. But Peter and the disciples were not ready for this. They wanted their own type of hero-messiah. And so Mark's Jesus reprimands them sternly (v. 33).

REFLECTION: Jesus asks us the same question he aasked his own disciples (in 33 A.D.) and the disciples of Mark (in 70 A.D.): "Who do *you* say that I am?" We can no longer look on as spectators. We are on the stage and he's asking us. Do we know our lines?

Jesus, Son of Man, you are the one who died out of love for all mankind. Inspire me with the courage to love you and others with the same intensity, unto the end!

COMMENT: After Jesus' dramatic revelation of *his* identity as the suffering Messiah-savior (vs. 31f.), he confronts "the crowd with his disciples" with *their* true identity as his followers (vs. 34-38). No longer do we hear Jesus speaking to Peter. Now, "If *a man* wishes to come after me . . ." (v. 34); "*Whoever* would preserve his life . . ." (v. 35); "What profit does *a man* show . . ." (v. 36); "What can *a man* offer in exchange for his life?" (v. 37). *Anyone* who wants to be Christ's follower, says Mark, must respond to the challenge! Will the Son of Man be ashamed of *you* when he comes? (v. 38).

REFLECTION: It is scary to surrender ourselves to another person, even to Jesus himself, when we know that the surrender will lead to the total gift of self. To the degree that Christians follow the Christ, they will love more and suffer more; they will see more of him and more of humanity; they will discover who he is and who they are.

Christ, you call for a total response from me. Here I am, Lord. Strengthen me. For I want to follow.

COMMENT: We pause here to reflect on this one verse, isolating it because of the questions it has raised through the centuries. For the words of Jesus, as reported here by Mark, seem to say quite clearly that Jesus was among those who thought the end of the world was coming in the very near future. Was he referring to the manifestation of his glory in the transfiguration (9:2-8)? Or to the coming of the Holy Spirit after his resurrection? Or was Jesus really fully human, even sharing the expectations of his contemporaries: that the final judgment and a completely new world order was about to supercede the world as he experienced it? Elsewhere in Mark's Gospel (1:15 and 13:30), it seems that the latter was truly the meaning of the early Christian traditions, and indeed, the understanding of Jesus himself!

REFLECTION: How can we admit that our Lord and Savior was mistaken? That he could have been wrong about the time of the coming of the kingdom (parousia)? Today we more readily accept the humanity of Jesus than we did a few years ago. We struggle to understand, with Mark, that the Lord our God indeed became like us *in all things,* except sin (read and pray Hebrews 4:15 & 2:17f.). As we base our lives on his, we are called to build up the Body of Christ, praying:

Lord Jesus, come in glory!

COMMENT: The favorite disciples of Jesus, the "intimates" who elsewhere in Mark's Gospel share in Jesus' most profound moments of earthly power (5:37-40) and earthly agony (14:33), are now led off alone by him. They are given insight into the transforming glory of Jesus which shall overcome his death. Mark places this vision of the glorious Jesus, the fulfiller of all the Law (Moses) and the Prophets (Elijah), right after the first of three predictions of Jesus' fate — the cross. This is a consoling vision, a necessary one for the weak disciples. However, Mark doesn't allow his disciples to drift off into awe-filled, unChristian, unrealistic hopes. For God speaks from the cloud: "This is my beloved Son; *listen* to him!" The Son has just spoken clearly of the cross (see 8:31-9:1), and he shall repeat the message again (see 9:30-32 and 10:32-34). His suffering is fully in accord with the Father's will. Listen!

REFLECTION: We long for peace and rest, for the end of all suffering and confusion. We shall experience the promised glory of God one day. With hope in the one who overcame death, because of his loving obedience and service of his Father, we pause and listen with the intimate disciples . . . only to be urged to move on with him on his way.

How good it is to draw strength from the Christian hope for eternal peace with God! Now, I look up and see before me only you, Jesus. Lead me.

COMMENT: Mark follows the glorious transfiguration (9:2-8) with another passage that accents the dullness of the Jesus' disciples. For they (in 30 A.D.) had problems in understanding why the glorious Son of Man had to rise from the dead (vs. 9-10). (Belief in the resurrection from the dead was widespread among the Jews of Jesus' day . . . it was its application to the Son of Man that puzzled them.) Mark stresses this because his Christians (in 70 A.D.) had the same problem in grasping the fullness of the Easter message: i.e. that Jesus' *death* was as essential to their salvation as was his resurrection! The Elijah dialogue (vs. 11-13) emphasizes the same thing: Elijah had already come in the person of John the Baptist, and he had been treated with contempt (see Mk 6:16ff.). The Son of Man (in the person of Jesus) also *had to suffer,* as the Scriptures had foretold!

REFLECTION: Mark's preoccupation with Christian suffering might seem to be a distorted obsession. However, a generous Christian, living the life of sacrificial love, will see the value of his or her own suffering in the light of the Christian hope, which promises the peace of the kingdom to those who suffer as their Lord did before them (see Mt 5:10-12).

Keep in mind that Jesus Christ has died for us and is risen from the dead. He is our saving Lord; he is joy for all ages!

COMMENT: This dramatic account of Jesus' expulsion of evil spirits is one of *only two* healing miracles in the second section of Mark's Gospel (8:27-13:37; the other cure is found in 10:46-52). The bulk of this part of the gospel is made up of Jesus' teachings about the grievous sufferings his true followers will have to endure in continuing his work, and their consequent need for total trust and commitment to him (e.g. 8:34-36 and 10:35-45). Thus Mark presents this moving account here, not so much to show how powerful Jesus was, but rather to emphasize the necessity for radical faith in the true Christian disciple. The disciples could not cure the boy (v. 18) because they did not consciously and prayerfully rely on God, as Jesus and the boy's father did (vs. 23 and 29)!

REFLECTION: All Christians are called to carry on Jesus' healing ministry in a world broken by sickness, sin, and solitude. But frustration and near despair set in when we fail and seem to have nothing to offer to the people we wish to console. Are not these the moments for union with the suffering servant whose life seemed to end in failure? In prayer, do we try to abandon ourselves to the Father's loving will and power?

Remove this cup from me; yet, not what I will, but what you will . . . I believe in you: help my unbelief.

COMMENT: As Jesus and his followers secretly move on their last trip to Jerusalem (v. 30), the second of three passion predictions suddenly rings out like a warning bell. (The first and third predictions appear in ch. 8 and ch. 10.) Mark inserts the second prediction here to assure his Christians that the Son of Man had no illusions about what would happen to him in Jerusalem (v. 31). But Mark's Christians also knew how the disciples had abandoned their Lord during his passion. How could this be? Why were they so blind and fearful, after he had prepared them by three predictions? In v. 32 Mark reconciles the disciples' fear-filled reaction to Jesus' death by saying that they really didn't understand what Jesus meant by his prediction, and that they were afraid to ask him.

REFLECTION: Our Christian life journey can often become tedious. Sometimes we find ourselves drifting for days or weeks without consciously choosing to stop, pray, and realize what Christian life is all about. Does Sunday Mass cause us to remember that we are Christ's followers? Are there special people, places, or things around us that can open our eyes and hearts daily to the presence of Jesus ahead of us on the road to our Jerusalem?

Jesus, Son of Man, make my journey be conformed to yours; a journey of sacrificial love unto life eternal!

COMMENT: These verses are the sequel to Jesus' second passion prediction, and are thus very important for our understanding of Mark's gospel challenge. They make all of Mark's readers concretely aware of what it means to be a disciple of Jesus, on *his* way: "If anyone would be first, he must be last of all and servant of all" (v. 35). Mark will follow the third prediction of Jesus' death with the same call to selfless service (see 10:35-45). It becomes obvious that for Jesus and for Mark, true Christianity and true greatness means humble service, not the vainglory of being "the greatest" (v. 34). In vs. 36-37, Mark's Jesus encourages Christians of all times: "Go out then, as my children and as humble servants. Then, when you preach the gospel, others will accept you as my true followers!"

REFLECTION: Mark's overshadowing message of the cross (chs. 8-16) takes on concrete meaning here for all of God's children: although there are few Christians who will be put to death on a cross (like some early martyrs), you and I can be among the many who die for others by serving them humbly in their need . . . in his name.

Lord, I want to be alert to the many opportunities I have this day to serve others "in your name."

COMMENT: Jesus has just made it clear that he wants his disciples to be humble servants (9:35). The disciples respond by moving from ambition (9:34) to arrogance (9:38): "we saw a man who was casting out demons in your name, and we forbade him because he was not following *us*." Mark's Jesus almost shouts out: "When will you blind and arrogant disciples finally understand what Christianity is all about?" It was true that the first disciples wanted to follow Jesus; but in their enthusiasm they failed to be tolerant and open to other men of good will. Mark tells his Christians through this section: "Working in Jesus' name is not reserved to a special few. Anyone who does so will receive his reward" (vs. 39-41).

REFLECTION: St. Paul spoke of some preachers in Philippi who preached Christ from motives of envy and rivalry: "Some act from unaffected love . . . others promote Christ, not from pure motives, but as an intrigue against me. What of it? All that matters is that in any and every way Christ is being proclaimed" (Phil 1:16-18). Is our involvement in the Christian apostolate as open-minded and as accepting of others as was Paul's and Jesus'?

Jesus, teach me to be more tolerant with those who serve you differently than I do; teach me to accept lovingly all people of good will!

COMMENT: Mark now chooses to present a series of Jesus' warning-sayings about "causing others to sin" (v. 42), about the "causes of sin" in oneself (vs. 43-8), and about some qualities needed by true disciples (vs. 49f.). The traditional biblical imagery used here ("to burn in the unquenchable fire," vs. 44-8) is designed to call up strong feelings of aversion and horror. In the face of such horror, our good example to others and the possession of God's kingdom are worth any sacrifice (even "to be drowned in the sea" v. 42, or "to cut off a hand or a foot" vs. 43f.). Mark thus urges his disciples, as Jesus did, to go to any lengths to "be at peace with one another" (v. 50).

REFLECTION: Who are the "little ones" that we hurt by our bad example? How much of God's gift of grace and faith in others have we frustrated by our sinful or insensitive remarks or actions? We ourselves are gifted Christians, the salt of the earth. What are we good for? What can each of us do this day to share the gift of God's grace and peace with one of his little ones? Shall we do it?

"O Savior, what a grace to be numbered among those whom you make use of to transfer your blessings to your Church!" (St. Vincent de Paul).

COMMENT: Here (in vs. 6-9) we find the original tradition about Jesus' attitude regarding the intimate and indissoluble union of man and woman in marriage. Jesus quotes Genesis 1:27 & 2:24 as his authority. His was a radical interpretation of the Law, in a Jewish society where men could divorce their wives for many and various "valid" reasons. In Jesus' own time, and later, his disciples were not certain that he really meant to be so strong with his words (v. 10). The early Church would develop his challenge into a rule for their community (vs. 11f.). Mark saw in this radical respect for the marriage union a practical way for his Christians to share in the "cup" which Jesus offered to all his followers (10:38f.).

REFLECTION: In our times, with the divorce rate so high, innumerable Christians struggle with the problems of broken homes, fatherless (or motherless) families, and the anger and guilt aroused by the words of Jesus: no divorce and remarriage without committing adultery! The Church struggles along with them. As the Church attempts to maintain the traditional respect for the marriage union, the Spirit is urging her to ask such questions as: "are there some marriages, even in Catholic ceremonies, that are not valid? What is God's will about marriage?"

Jesus, spouse of your people, be with all people: single or married, divorced or separated. And protect your children who want to respond to you.

COMMENT: Perhaps it was the mention of marriage (10:2-12) that reminded Mark of Jesus' human and tender love for the child. (Only Mark records that Jesus was "indignant" with the disciples who rebuked the parents: see Matt 19:14; only Mark's Jesus embraces the children before blessing them: see Matt 19:15.) But more than likely, Mark places this section here because of the great need that all Christians have for childlike trust and receptivity, as they long for God's kingdom. A child will follow his parents into the dark because he trusts them and knows they will keep him safe. In the midst of the radical demands of Christian discipleship, Jesus calls for the simplicity and trust of the child, who is content with depending on another's care.

REFLECTION: What a sad thing it is to hear someone say: "I don't need anyone. I can take care of myself." When we hear this or become aware of such an attitude in ourselves or in others, our Father asks us to consider the child: unself-conscious, receptive, and ready to follow a loving parent's lead. Even as adults, we are still his children. We need our Father to care for us. He does!

Father, your weak disciple often gets tired in the pursuit of your kingdom. Embrace me, your child, with your tender care and loving gifts.

COMMENT: "If you want to follow me to everlasting life, you have to do more than keep the commandments. You have to sell what you have and give it to the poor. Then you can come after me." There are no "if's" about it (see Matt 19:21). The disciple of Jesus is one who is completely detached from everything (and everyone, vs. 29-31); he is totally attached to Jesus and the kingdom. The man whom Jesus loved (v. 21) came to stand for any Christian in the early Church who thought that attachment to riches and Christianity were compatible. They weren't compatible (vs. 23-25). They still aren't. "It may seem impossible to give up all for the sake of Jesus and the gospel; but with God all things are possible, and you will receive a hundredfold for following him." (vs. 26ff.)

REFLECTION: Jesus' call to discipleship is radical. Today, just as in the first century, wealth means status, security and enjoyment in life. But this is precisely why Jesus' demand is so important today. For the essence of the Christian faith still is to rely solely on God as the source of security and well-being. Are we not among those searching for life and God? Can we allow ourselves to hear the enticing challenge to give up our security for Jesus, in the service of God's poor?

It seems so impossible, Jesus. But you look on me with love and tell me it IS possible, when I rely on you alone. Love your poor through me.

COMMENT: In this third and final prediction of his death and resurrection (see 8:31 and 9:31), Jesus adds the details that "the Gentiles (Romans) will mock him, spit upon hom, scourge him, and kill him" (vs. 33f.). Mark adds a more significant detail, as he describes the setting of the prediction (v. 32): Jesus walks *ahead* of his disciples, going up to Jerusalem: he *consciously* accepts his destiny. They "follow in amazement, and the rest of the crowd follows in fear." Where are they going? Jesus shares with the twelve that they go to his death: the cross. The cross! The cross! For the third time, the cross! (But after three days he shall rise, v. 34.) Can the early Christians accept his destiny as theirs?

REFLECTION: Hosea spoke of the third day on which God would raise up Israel to live with him, *after* he had struck them down (Hosea 6:1-2). Second Isaiah spoke of the Suffering Servant "who bore our infirmities, was crushed for our sins, and by whose scourgings we were healed" (Isa 53:4ff.). Jesus is the Suffering Servant. Yet we still face the cross of suffering in every church, as we worship his glory. When will we see that it is through such a loving death for others that we will come to the joy and peace of Christian life?

Lord Jesus, suffering servant, with all of burdened humanity I cry out: lead me on your way!

COMMENT: The "cup" mentioned in vs. 38f. is a key word in the Christian message of Mark. The cup Jesus will choose in the garden (14:36) is the same cup every Christian partakes of at the Eucharist (14:23f.). It is the cup of suffering and the baptism of pain that any Christian shares in when he or she chooses to love as Jesus did. What a contrast to the ambitions of James and John (vs. 35-41)! Yet, when other Christians (like the "other ten" in v. 41 and those in the early Church) scold the ambitious brothers, Jesus applies a general principle to all: "*Whoever* would be great among you can become the greatest only by serving the needs of all . . . by serving like the Son of Man, who gave his life as a ransom for many" (vs. 42ff.). Mark asked his Christians: "Do you want to be true Christians? Do you choose to live for others?"

REFLECTION: There is no short cut to the kingdom. As the Teacher goes, so goes the Teacher's disciple. How does your parish prove itself to be a living witness of the Servant Christ and the Servant Church? Is there any group that truly empties itself for others? How can you assist your priests in making the local Church a more loving Servant of God's people, a living sign of the kingdom?

Because I am a Christian, I wish from now on to become the first to seek, to sympathize, and to suffer; the first to sacrifice myself for others.

COMMENT: The cure of blind Bartimaeus is another "key" section of Mark's Gospel (see comment on 8:27-28). Until the resurrection (16:1-8), it is the *last* miracle that Jesus is involved in. Mark asks of his early Christians the same trust that Jesus received from Bartimaeus: "Son of David, have mercy on me" (vs. 47f.). Whereas the blind man in 8:22-26 was cured "in stages" and was sent away to his home (8:26), Bartimaeus "immediately received his sight and followed him on the way" (v. 52). After the difficult teachings of Jesus about the Christian attitude toward divorce, riches, and ambition (ch. 10), this miracle story is placed here by Mark to encourage his early Christians to trust in the Lord's power to cure them in their weakness on *their own* way of the cross! "Take heart; rise, he is calling *you*" (v. 49).

REFLECTION: How blind we can be at times! How frustrated in our attempts to live and preach Christ's message of selfless lóve for others. Indeed, Jesus came to relieve our blindness and suffering. When we see him hanging on our crucifixes, do we see that we are invited to be healed and to heal others by that same sort of loving gift of ourselves?

Master, let me receive my sight; let me follow you with eyes wide open, on your demanding but loving way!

COMMENT: "Shout for joy, O daughter Jerusalem! See, your king shall come to you; a just savior is he, meek, and riding on the foal of an ass!" (Zechariah 9:9). "Blessed is he who comes in the name of the Lord! O Lord, grant salvation! Hosanna!" (Psalm 118:25f.). These cries of prophet and psalmist were cries of joy which the early Christians saw fulfilled in Jesus' entry into Jerusalem. For them he was the long-awaited Savior, says Mark (vs. 7-10). But when we carefully compare Mark's account with Matthew's version (Matt 21:1-17), we see that Mark plays down the reaction of the crowds to the coming of their "king." For Mark will not permit his believers to forget that Jesus is the one who has been led to Jerusalem to save them by his very "unkingly" crucifixion.

REFLECTION: It is not by accident that there are two gospels read at the Palm Sunday liturgy, which commemorates Jesus' entry into Jerusalem. After the triumphal arrival (Mk 11:1-11) comes the passion account (14:1-15:47). It is exhilarating and easy to cheer for a popular and winning team; but are we dogged followers of Christ, uniting ourselves with him, even in the depths of frustration and failure?

Christ, I want to know you and the power of your Resurrection: I also want to share in your sufferings. Thus will I arrive at the Resurrection from the dead (Philippians 3:10-11).

COMMENT: Two of the strangest stories about Jesus are here "sandwiched together," in a manner reminiscent of the way Mark combined two miracle stories in 5:21-43. The whole section should be read, for the meaning of one story depends on the other. The uncharacteristic action of Jesus regarding the fig tree (vs. 12-14 & 20f.) seems to symbolize the tragic fate in store for Jerusalem and the Jewish religion. (See the prophecies of Jeremiah 8:13 and Micah 7:1-6.) This symbolic parable thus sheds light on the meaning of the cleansing of the Temple (vs. 15-17), which is woven into the fig tree account. Upon Jesus' approach to the Temple, he sees the place of prayer "for all the nations" (v. 17) being used for unholy purposes. He judges their temple practice as mere ceremonial foliage, containing no real fruit of holiness. Mark concludes this section with related sayings on the power of true prayer and the need for forgiveness in one who prays (vs. 22ff.).

REFLECTION: In these "strange" sections of Mark's Gospel, could God be urging us to reflect on the sincerity of our own prayer life and religious practices, as individuals and as Church today?

Lord, cleanse my heart and make me a worthy dwelling place for your Spirit.

COMMENT: The hostile reaction to all of Jesus' activity (including the cleansing of the Temple, 11:15ff.) becomes evident again when Jesus returns to Jerusalem (v. 27). In the city of his death, the conflict motif of Jesus' early ministry (see 2:1-3:6) reaches a new peak! The Jewish authorities question his authority to teach and act as he does (v. 28), and this challenge leads to more episodes of conflict (in ch. 12). Mark's Christians must have been encouraged by Jesus, as he outwitted the trained experts of Judaism (vs. 29-33), silencing them with his clever counter-question about John the Baptist's activity and teaching (v. 30). Through this first encounter of conflict (just prior to the ultimate conflict with death) Mark shows that Jesus' authority *is* from God! (See 16:6).

REFLECTION: Our modern Church has often been described as "the Church in conflict." In this difficult time of renewal, as in Jesus' time, it is appropriate to question those who serve God's people in their positions of authority; but it is also vital that people and pastor, priest and bishop dialogue together and discern God's way with sincere hearts and open minds, not hedging and fearing what others might say or do (v. 32).

Lord Jesus, make me open and fearless in my attempts to discern your way in the renewal of your people!

COMMENT: Mark follows a story of conflict between Jesus and the Jewish authorities with this allegorical interpretation of the parable of the wicked hired-hands. It is clear from v. 12 that Mark and the early Church saw the Jewish leaders in the parable as the evil keepers of the vineyard. It was they (not "the multitude") who put the "beloved son" to death (vs. 6-8). The other servants, who were beaten and/or killed (vs. 3-5), obviously represented the prophets sent to Israel by its God. And Jesus is the one rejected by Israel, the one who has become the cornerstone of a new building of faith, the church (vs. 10f., which apply Psalm 118 to Jesus). As Jesus' death draws near, Mark makes it clear where the blame for it lay.

REFLECTION: What a dramatic indictment of the Jewish leaders! Whether or not Mark was challenging the leaders of his church to see if they too were rejecting Jesus *in their day,* we must read this passage as just such a challenge. As Mark says in 9:35f.: "If anyone would be first, he must be last of all and servant of all . . . whoever receives a little child in my name receives me." And whoever rejects one such child. . . .

My sacrifice is a contrite spirit, O God; a heart contrite and humbled, you will not spurn. Be bountiful to Zion in your kindness, by rebuilding the walls of Jerusalem! (Psalm 51)

COMMENT: Mark continues the interchange between Jesus and the Jewish leadership with this story that concerns paying tribute to Caesar. The leaders came to trap Jesus in his talk (says Mark in v. 13), but they present themselves as God-fearing Jews concerned with a very real issue in Jesus' day: could they pay taxes to Caesar, or was that against the Law of Moses? (vs. 14f.). Jesus' classic response to the trouble-makers is more than a witty, evasive answer. It "amazed them" because it was direct and to the point. Moreover, it seems to have been the norm which the early Church followed in similar crises of conscience (see especially Romans 13:3-7). Mark's innocent Jesus has passed yet another test; it is obvious that he was a good Jew, undeserving of either Roman *or* Jewish punishment "as a rebel"!

REFLECTION: We pause with Mark to marvel at the wisdom and innocence of our crucified Lord. When we are challenged because of our convictions, even by those who seem to be "out to get us," do we seek the help of the Lord and his Spirit? Do we respond directly and in truth? Or do we falter and hedge, compromising our principles? Surely his wisdom far surpasses ours. But does our courage even begin to approximate his?

Wise and courageous Lord, be with me in moments of conflict, especially when there is a question of YOUR truth and YOUR gospel involved!

COMMENT: This strange encounter brings the Sadducees into Mark's Gospel for the first and only time. Did he introduce them so that Jesus could be seen as maintaining his orthodoxy against them, as well as against the Pharisaic wing of Judaism? Whether or not this was Mark's intention, the Sadducees were known for their lack of belief in the resurrection (v. 15); and in this passage Mark's Jesus responds forcefully to their legalistic argumentation about one of Moses' marriage laws (v. 19, quoting Deuteronomy 25:5). Reminding them how God told Moses that he was "the God of Abraham, Isaac, and Jacob" (v. 26), he uses acceptable rabbinic argumentation to prove that the Sadducees do *not* know their scripture and do *not* appreciate the power of God to overcome death and to give a new form of life after death (vs. 24f.).

REFLECTION: Although Jesus' response (vs. 24-27) might not sound very clear or convincing to modern day readers of this passage, it was evidently sufficient to stand as a first century explanation and proof of survival after death. Do we know what the scriptures say about death and resurrection today? A prayerful reading of Paul's First Letter to the Corinthians, 15:35-58, is a good passage to reflect on in this regard.

Lord, I trust in you. You will show me the path to life, fullness of joys in your presence, delights at your right hand forever (Ps. 16).

COMMENT: The rather friendly dialogue between Jesus and one of the scribes seems almost "out of place" in this context of Jesus' conflicts with the Pharisees, Herodians, and Sadducees. Jesus has triumphantly responded to their hostile testing and has shown his faithfulness to the Law. Now the scribe recognizes in Jesus' response the authentic voice of Israel's great prophets: Moses, who gave God's commands of love to Israel (vs. 29-31; Deuteronomy 6:2 and Leviticus 19:18); Samuel and Hosea, who declared that love was worth more than any burnt offerings (v. 33; 1 Samuel 15:22 and Hosea 6:6). Notice how the questioning scribe (in v. 28) becomes the wise student of the kingdom (in v. 34). Indeed, *no one* can question the orthodoxy and wisdom of Jesus, the Teacher who draws all to the kingdom of God!

REFLECTION: Meditation upon this episode might turn our thoughts to the passages in Paul and John about the *one* Christian commandment to "love one another as I have loved you." But let's allow ourselves to marvel here at how thoroughly Jewish Jesus was. By doing so, we can rejoice in the fact of his humanity, rooted in the history of the Jewish people. Our Lord is the God of history: who spoke with Moses and who speaks with us today!

Lord of all mankind, I want to love you and my neighbor with all my heart, soul, mind and strength. Draw me to your kingdom of love!

COMMENT: "Whose son is 'the Messiah' (i.e., 'the Christ') ?" The answer given by the scribes of Jesus' day was simply and unhesitatingly: "The Christ is the son of David!" (v. 35). But Jesus is reported as challenging this common belief by quoting David himself (Psalm 110:1), and then asking: "How could the Messiah be David's son if David himself calls him Lord?" (v. 37). Mark's Church knew that Jesus *was* the Messiah (=Christ) and that he was of Davidic descent; but they also believed more . . . that he was the Son of God! And so the question left hanging by Jesus calls for that "something more" in Mark's church; a renewal of their commitment in faith to Jesus, the Christ, as the true Son of God!

REFLECTION: In our personal prayer and in our common liturgical worship we call upon Jesus as Lord, Christ, Savior, etc. We acknowledge him as the Son of David and the Son of God. All of these exalted titles are his due. But at this moment in our reading of Mark's Gospel, God the Father challenges us to renew our faith commitment to his son, Jesus Christ, who died out of love for us and whose example stands before all others who bear the name of Christ!

Father, transform me into a worthy son. May I say with St. Paul: "I live now, no longer I, but Christ lives in me" (Galatians 2:21).

Comment: Now that Mark has proven Jesus victorious in his interchanges with the scribes (vs. 28-37), he gives a final warning against their pretentious religious practices (vs. 38-40). In Mark's day, some forty years after Jesus' death and resurrection, this warning would have been intended for *anyone* who put on false, religious airs (vs. 38f.), while acting unjustly, even with defenseless widows (v. 40)!

Reflection: When we hear Mark's Jesus contrast the piety of the scribes with their lack of concern for the widows, we hear the chords of a familiar melody played throughout the ages of the Jewish-Christian tradition. For Moses had followed his commands about sacrifices to the Lord with "you shall not wrong any widow or orphan or stranger. If ever you wrong them and they cry out to me, I will surely hear their cry!" (Exodus 22:19ff.). The Epistle of James sums it up this way: "Religion that is pure and undefiled before God is this: to visit orphans and widows in their affliction, and to keep oneself unstained from the world" (James 1:27). Is our worship of God in church characterized by our living concern for God's needy ones?

Lord, when the just cry out, you hear them, and from all their distress you rescue them. Help me worship you purely by loving your needy children!

COMMENT: Mark dramatically contrasts Jesus' warning against the pretentious "scribes who devour widows' houses" (12:40) with this famous story of the generous, poor widow. It is an apt transition to Jesus' last discourse (ch. 13) and to the account of how Jesus "gave everything" for us (chs. 14-15). The point of this story is as clear for Mark's disciples in 70 A.D. as it was for Jesus' own disciples: to enter the kingdom of God as a true follower of Jesus, it is necessary to give of your whole self, without reserve; if one is less generous, he or she is not really taking Jesus seriously.

REFLECTION: This little story is among the most memorable and touching sections of the gospels. In its simplicity, the contrast between the wealthy contributors and the poor widow immediately drives home its point: Christian discipleship is expressed by the gift of self, not by the money we drop in the basket. It is significant to realize that widows (along with orphans and strangers) were the ones whom God especially cared for in the Hebrew scriptures (e.g., Exodus 22:21; Deut 24:17ff.). Perhaps we might learn from them what God's care really is . . . and what it means to depend solely on God and to respond to him with the totality of our lives.

Lord, you changed my mourning into dancing: you clothed me with gladness. O Lord, my God, forever will I give you thanks (Psalm 30).

COMMENT: Jesus' last extended speech to his disciples concerns the destruction of the majestic temple in Jerusalem (vs. 1-4), which he closely relates to the signs which would precede the end of the world (vs. 5-13). In the years after Jesus' death, famine and earthquakes *did* occur. The temple *was* destroyed by the Romans in 70 A.D., after various Jewish rebellions in Palestine against Roman rule. And some of these revolts had been hailed by religious fanatics as the coming of the kingdom (vs. 5-8). During all this, the young Christian faith was held suspect (v. 9), and even families were divided (v. 13), "for the sake of Jesus' name." Mark presents Jesus' words to his people in the alarming situation of 70 A.D. to provide, not a message of doom and fear, but one of calm hope and perseverance in faith: "Be on guard and don't panic . . . The Holy Spirit will be with you to the end, as you preach the good news to all mankind."

REFLECTION: Although first century Christians were mistaken about the world coming to an end very soon, they were not wrong in encouraging calm and persevering hope in a time of crisis. The Spirit is still with us today as we witness the horrors of war and hatred, as we hear the false witnesses of doom, and as we are held in contempt for our beliefs.

Father, bless me with your peace today, and make me a living sign of love and hope that will bring all to you.

COMMENT: We now read more of the "apocalypse" (i.e. "revelation") chapter in Mark's Gospel. The revelation about the "desolating sacrilege" (vs. 14ff.) was purposely presented in this form because it would have been too dangerous for the Christians to say directly: "the Romans are oppressing us now (forcing us to worship their emperors as gods, vs. 14-18); and others are trying to lead us astray (claiming that the end of the world is here, vs. 19f.); but our Lord will protect us from them all. He will warn us with signs and wonders (vs. 24f.), and only then will he come as the Son of Man to gather all his elect to himself (vs. 26f.)." In this manner Mark builds up the hope of his oppressed community, while at the same time encouraging them to remain courageous and to see God's protection through all that is happening to them.

REFLECTION: Jesus came to bring his kingdom of love and peace into the lives of men. He will also return "in those final days" to establish his kingdom in glory. Many people falsely interpret the natural catastrophes and moral decadence of our times as the signs of doom preceding the end. Through Mark, God urges us to stay clear of *all* false prophets. His true message remains: "Take heed, watch and pray" (13:33).

Lord, increase my trust in your protecting love.

COMMENT: As the blossoming fig tree points to the coming of summer, Mark's Christians are urged to be ready for the proximate coming of the Lord (13: 4-24, 28-30; see *Comment* on 9:1). But then there is a sudden shift in the whole tone of this discourse. In vs. 32-37, Jesus is no longer pictured as one who would reveal signs of the end. Now the time of the end is completely unknown to anyone except the Father (v. 32). Now Mark's Christians are urged to live as watchful servants who will have *no* warning or sign of the master's return (vs. 34f.). Suddenly the private revelation to Peter and the others (13:3) becomes a moral lesson for *all* Christians: "Wait without impatience; but watch, pray, and be ready at every moment; for you do not know the time" (vs. 33-37).

REFLECTION: The early Church was very conscious of the absence of their Lord. They longed for his return and perhaps had begun to place all their hope in his future coming. While our hopes for our peaceful, eternal union with him are not to be abandoned, we too are called to live in the present. We each have our daily service (v. 34) to offer to the Lord and to his people. We too are called to do our work alertly and prayerfully (vs. 33-37).

May the Lord of peace bless all his people with peace at all times in all ways (2 Thessalonians 3:16).

COMMENT: In these verses we have the introduction to the Passion narrative (chs. 14-15) in Mark's Gospel. It is generally agreed that the passion story existed in Christian circles before Mark wrote. Read in liturgical celebrations, it dramatically presented the sacrificial love of Jesus that saved all men. Then Mark appropriated the traditional passion account, making it the apt conclusion of his good news (see *Comment* on 1:1). In this brief introduction to the passion, Jesus is portrayed as the one whom the chief priests were trying to kill (vs. 1f.), whom Judas would betray (vs. 10f.), and who deserves the honor and devotion due to a Messiah (vs. 3-9). "Anyone who reads the events that follow this woman's action," implies Mark, "must see them as the greatest act of the Anointed One, our Messiah!"

REFLECTION: Lord, your disciples still failed to understand your role as Suffering Servant (vs. 4f.). As we recall the devotion you aroused in the woman who anointed you, we want to understand your gracious love of humanity. We want to hear your call to serve you today; and we honor you by revering your body as it lives and breathes in the poor we have with us (v. 7).

Jesus, I want to be a faithful follower. Make your Good News burn in my heart like a fire. Let my life be like a song of praise — for you have rescued the life of the poor man from death!

COMMENT: In relating this incident, the early Christian community proclaimed that Jesus was the Messiah, the only one who could possess such supernatural insight. Not only was Jesus reported as foretelling the disciples' meeting with the man with the water jug (v. 13); the man also complied with his wishes immediately by leading them to a furnished room (vs. 15f.). Two other details should be noted here. First this is the only passage in the passion narrative that explicitly says that the meal to follow would be the Jewish Passover meal (vs. 12, 14, 16). Secondly, Jesus' supernatural foresight closely resembles that of the prophet Samuel, who sent Saul off to meet two men near Rachel's tomb . . . and he predicted that Saul would "save his people from the grasp of their enemies" (1 Samuel 10). "Thus, Jesus truly was the Messiah," says Mark. "And the meal to follow this episode was surely one of great significance for all people!"

REFLECTION: This extraordinary prelude to Jesus' last meal with his disciples highlights the Messiah's foreknowledge and authority over what was about to happen to him. Our preparation for the eucharistic meal should be full of trust in the Lord.

As I approach your altar, Lord, make me aware of your victory over death. Help me to celebrate your life-giving sacrifice in total trust!

COMMENT: Throughout Mark's Gospel Jesus has been in conflict with the Pharisees. With the same intensity, Mark has characterized the disciples as being blind to Jesus' purpose in life (especially in chs. 6-10). Now an unnamed disciple (Judas will be named explicitly in the arrest scene in 14:43) is singled out as the one to bring about the final conflict (vs. 18-20). The allusion to Psalm 41:9 (in v. 18) brings out the horrible fact that "even my bosom friend in whom I trusted, who ate of my bread, has lifted his heel against me." In 70 A.D. were there conflicts, misunderstanding, and even betrayal plaguing Mark's young Christian community? If there were, they were truly horrible, and "woe to the persons causing them" (v. 21).

REFLECTION: Christians partake of the Body of Christ weekly, and even daily, at the Eucharistic table. Yet we know that we are a sinful people, often doing harm to members of Christ's Body by failing to love them in our daily lives. We misunderstand others and are often the cause of serious conflicts after we leave our churches. Mark's Jesus asks us: "You who call yourselves my disciples — do you express in your lives my concrete love of others? Or do you lift your heel against me?"

Jesus, soften my hardened heart and make me your faithful disciple, unto the end.

COMMENT: The Eucharistic meal has always been at the heart of Christian community life. Yet, beginning with the days of St. Paul and St. Mark, Christians have failed to grasp the full meaning of the Eucharist. Mark had carefully shown the close relationship between bread and the passion of Jesus in the feeding stories (chs. 6-8). Now he emphasizes that the bread is Christ's body, which has been prepared for burial (14:8,22). This Christian meal is truly a foretaste of the heavenly banquet we shall share with Jesus in the kingdom of God (v. 25); but it is also the Christian's present opportunity to share intimately in the loving life, death, and resurrection of Jesus. "Take the cup, but don't fail to see your sharing of my cross as you drink of it . . . for it is the blood of the covenant, poured out for many," meant to establish a new intimate relationship with God (v. 25).

REFLECTION: Mark asks us to do more than "receive communion" at the Eucharist. He asks us to become one with Jesus and to "go out with him to the Mount of Olives" (v. 26). Mark calls for more than our "attendance" at Mass. He calls for our active participation in Christ's concern to bring all people into the new intimate relationship with his Father, which he established by his loving death.

My Lord and My God, may my communion with you be a loving witness of your sacrificial love for all the sons and daughters of our Father.

COMMENT: Several sayings of Jesus here foretell:
1) Jesus' suffering and the consequent dispersion
of his disciples (v. 27); 2) his appearance in Galilee
after the resurrection (v. 28); and 3) the denial of
Peter (vs. 29-31). The sayings were probably meant
to show the early Christian believers that Jesus' sufferings were in accord with Old Testament prophecies (cf. Zechariah 13:7) and that Jesus had some
supernatural insight into the Father's power to raise
him from the dead (see 16:7). Moreover, even
though Peter and the others will not stay with him
until the end, they do believe in Jesus enthusiastically
(see 14:38, "the spirit is willing, but the flesh is
weak;" see also 14:66-72).

REFLECTION: As we read these verses today, we
could join the first readers of the gospel and say:
"Poor Peter! He really thought he would go to death
with Jesus before denying him! And look at what
happened!" However, in order to respond fully to
God's word, isn't it more appropriate to ask ourselves: "When we experience tensions and problems
this very day, will we meet them with the Christian
hope of resurrection? Will we hear Jesus challenging
us to unite our sufferings to his loving sacrifice for
all men?"

**Have pity on me, O God, for men trample upon me:
O Most High, when I begin to fear, in you will I
trust (Psalm 56).**

COMMENT: The emotionally charged and moving "Gethsemane scene" is actually made up of two scenes, leaving a double impact upon Mark's readers. The first scene focuses on Jesus' own turmoil (vs. 33-36). He who earlier had affirmed with conviction and authority that he would suffer, die and be raised up now falters and "is greatly distressed and troubled" (v. 33). His profound humanity emerges in solitary prayer, as he expresses his desire to bypass the cup and hour of ultimate suffering (vs. 36-36). His voluntary acceptance of his Father's will (the cup, v. 36) is the ultimate proof of his love for his Father and for all men. The second scene focuses on the weak, sleeping disciples (vs. 37-41). Three times he must awake and rebuke them. Mark's disciples in 70 A.D. were much like the three disciples of Jesus. They too had to wake up and come to terms with the scandal of the passion and death involved in following Jesus in their own circumstances.

REFLECTION: We can easily hear God speaking to us weak and tired Christians today when Mark's Jesus says: "let us be going; see, my betrayer is at hand" (v. 42). We falter in the painful moments of our Christian and human existence. Shall we meet *our* "hour" with Jesus' selfless love for us?

Abba, Father, all things are possible for you; remove this cup from me; yet not what I will, but what you will (v. 36).

COMMENT: Jesus is betrayed by a friend's kiss (vs. 44f.). Yet, Jesus was neither a robber (v. 48) nor a revolutionary teacher who had anything to hide (v. 49). As the innocent one is led away, he makes it clear that what was happening here was according to God's will (v. 49), just like all the events of the passion were in accordance with Old Testament predictions. Mark also passes on three details from tradition about Jesus' arrest that accent the superficial enthusiasm and faith of the disciples. One disciple thought he could save his Lord by violence (v. 47). All the others abandoned him (v. 50), as he had foretold (14:27). Even the young man who followed behind in the linen cloth soon ran away (v. 52). In relating these details, Mark would also have his own Christian disciples in mind: Is your involvement with the humiliated Lord superficial or deep? Will you follow?

REFLECTION: Christian discipleship costs. "Whoever would save his life will lose it; and whoever loses his life for my sake and the gospel's will save it" (8:35). In what existential situation in our individual lives is Jesus asking us to give our whole selves for his sake? What keeps us from being totally his? Will we follow?

"I desire neither death nor life. I only will what you will, and I am pleased with whatever you do. In my deepest suffering you will be here" (St. Therese of Lisieux).

COMMENT: The trial narrative in Mark's Gospel is full of irony. At the same time that Jesus' enemies are mocking him (v. 65) and accusing him of being a false prophet (vs. 57f.) Peter stands in the courtyard (v. 54), ready to deny him as he had prophesied (14:30). In a court of justice, the just one (v. 55) is testified against by false witnesses (v. 56). However, this passage is also full of hope. For the silent one *does* finally respond to the high priest's crucial question "Are you the Christ, the Son of the Blessed?" (v. 61). "I am," says the Marcan Jesus. "For the suffering of the Son of Man is not his end. Nor is suffering and death the end for the Christian. The Christ's way to death is really his way to life eternal. And so it is for the Marcan Christian."

REFLECTION: As Christians of twentieth century America, we do not live in daily fear of a Roman power hostile to our very existence. Although we are not persecuted for our faith as Mark's community was, we still need to hear his call to radical faith and hope. For we too suffer the agony of God's sons, longing for "the glorious liberty of the children of God," which will be ours when he comes again "with the clouds of heaven" (v. 62; see Romans 8:18ff.).

Holy Spirit, intercede for us. Help us to suffer with Christ in order that we may also be glorified with him! (See Romans 8:16f.).

READING Mark 14:66-72

COMMENT: The drama of Mark's passion narrative reaches a tearful climax, as Peter breaks down and weeps (v. 72). He has denied his Lord three times, just as Jesus had foretold (see 14:30). However, the members of the early Church knew very well that Peter's tears would turn into repentance, and that he would assume a major role in spreading the gospel of Jesus after the resurrection (see Galatians 2:6-10). Thus, in their own moments of doubt and confusion, Mark's Christians could relate well to Peter's sin of cowardice and still recall that he did not lose his faith because of it (compare this with the fate of Judas in Matt 27:5).

REFLECTION: We all refuse to admit that we are followers of Jesus at one time or another: when we add our cynical comments to an uncharitable conversation about an acquaintance; when we abandon him when he is in need in our sick, elderly, or bothersome brothers and sisters. It is never too late to turn to him with a contrite heart. It is never too late to say: "Yes, I am with Jesus of Nazareth!"

Jesus of Nazareth, I belong to you. In my weak faith I turn to you and proclaim my love for you in my loving acceptance of those who need me.

COMMENT: Jesus is questioned by the Roman leader, Pontius Pilate, after the Jewish leaders had "delivered him up" (v. 2). This particular choice of wording, plus Jesus' silence during the interrogation (v. 5), must have reminded Mark's Christians of the prophecies of Isaiah: "The Lord delivered him up for our sins. Though he was harshly treated, he submitted and opened not his mouth" (Isaiah 53:6f.). The early Christian community would have thus seen the accusing chief priests (v. 3) as the ones responsible for their Lord's death. They would have also seen the Jews in some mysterious way as the actors God chose to "deliver up" his suffering servant for the salvation of all people.

REFLECTION: History tells us that there was much hostility between Christians and Jews in the years immediately following the death and resurrection of Jesus. That Christian hostility comes through clearly in this passage (as it does in 15:6-15 and in the passion narratives of all four gospels), as Mark places the blame for Jesus' death squarely on the shoulders of the Jews. When we perpetuate anti-Semitic prejudice and hostility in the history that we are making today, we are no longer worthy of the name "Christian." For by doing so, we deny the basic Christian belief that:

"Lord, by your cross, you reconciled Jew and Gentile, making us both one in yourself" (Ephesians 2:14-16). Make me an instrument of your peace!

Comment: In the "Barabbas incident," as in the previous passage (15:1-5), Mark expresses the early Christian community's conviction that it was the Jews who were "the guilty ones" (vs. 10-11). They were the ones who asked for the release of the murderer Barabbas and for the crucifixion of Jesus, while the Roman authority wondered "what evil Jesus had done" (vs. 11-14). Yet Mark and his Christians could not deny that the people-pleasing Pilate had the last word and "delivered Jesus up" to the terrible flogging that preceded crucifixion (v. 15). And so Pilate joined the Jews as one of the actors God chose to direct in his divine drama of redemption (see *Comment* on 15:1-5).

Reflection: Most Christians have unfortunately grown up in the faith, uninformed about the long tradition of Christian anti-semitism and the bitter persecutions of Jews by Christians. Today it is vital that we not continue to make the mistake of blaming the whole Jewish people (of 33 A.D. or of today) for Jesus' death. Since we still sin, the cry "crucify him" is our cry. Ours too is the hope of the great Jewish prophet, Isaiah: "From one new moon to another, and from one sabbath to another, all mankind shall worship before him" (66:23).

Lord, as a member of your family, I hopefully join all people who await the day when we will address you and serve you with one accord!

COMMENT: When this episode is read merely as a report of "the way things happened," it causes feelings of pity for Jesus and contempt for the Roman soldiers. But Mark and his Christians would have understood far more in it. They would understand the mocking cry "Hail, king of the Jews" (v. 18) as *the truth* of the matter: Jesus truly was their king, and the king of all! They would see in Jesus the faithful "suffering servant" of Isaiah 50: "I gave my back to those who beat me . . . my face I did not shield from buffets and spitting" (v. 19). Their hopes would have been built up in their own suffering by seeing in Jesus the one "who endured *our* suffering . . . the one pierced for *our* offenses . . . by whose stripes *we* were healed" (Isaiah 53:4-6).

REFLECTION: Jesus does not want our pity for what happened long ago. Nor does he rejoice in our contempt for those who mocked him. He *does* want us to be merciful to the suffering and wounded members of his Mystical Body today. Through St. Paul he appeals to us to "let our love be genuine, outdoing one another in showing honor . . . even blessing those who persecute us" (Romans 12). A prayerful reading of Romans 12 might bring us into closer union with the one "they led out to crucify."

Lord Jesus, make me a living sacrifice of love, holy and acceptable to your Father. Teach me to love as you did.

Comment: As Mark relates Jesus' way of the cross and the crucifixion, the modern day Christian reader might well wonder why some familiar details are missing. For example, there is no good thief here as in Luke's Gospel (Lk 23:39ff.); and there is no mention of Jesus' "tunic without seam, woven from top to bottom" (Jn 19:23). Such details were added later for specific purposes by the evangelists who wrote after Mark. But Mark's first readers would be encouraged by his major point of emphasis in the crucifixion account: that Jesus' crucifixion truly was the fulfillment of God's will, foretold in Psalm 22 and Isaiah 53. "They look on me and gloat over me; they cast lots for my garments"; "he surrendered himself to death and was counted among the wicked." The seeming tragedy of the cross was thus understood as a part of God's plan for saving mankind!

Reflection: Why did Jesus have to go through all this? Why did his Father allow it? Why do the poor and the sick have to go through their daily misery? Why does God allow the innocent to suffer? Such questions are asked by sincere and discerning Christians. The answer, says St. Paul, lies in the wisdom of God, that is, in Christ crucified (1 Corinthians 1:18ff.) out of love for others.

Jesus, help me be more aware of being a member of the Body of Christ; and teach me to love as you did, in the school of suffering.

COMMENT: "On that day, says the Lord God, I will make the sun set at midday and cover the earth with darkness in broad daylight" (v. 33; cf. Amos 8:9). As the prophet Amos' words are fulfilled, Mark has Jesus speak *only one* sentence from the cross: "My God, my God, why have you forsaken me?" (v. 34; contrast this with John 19:25-30). Jesus' words are the cry of the innocent sufferer who trusts that he will be delivered (from Psalm 22). Mark goes on to interpret Jesus' death as the end of the Jewish temple religion (v. 38), for *they* are the ones who have abandoned him (implied in last part of v. 36). Moreover, Jesus' death brings about the profession of faith of the unbelieving gentile soldier: "Truly this man was the Son of God" (v. 39; see *Comment* on 1:1). His disciples are not there as he dies. It is the gentile and the women who are present to speak loudly and clearly to Christians of all times (vs. 39-41).

REFLECTION: Precisely in the humiliating death and failure of Jesus does the true Christian believer understand the divine love and victory of God over weakness of all kinds! The "good news" of St. Mark is not only that Jesus can cure sickness; it is most significantly the message of God's sacrificial and total love for us weak sinners (Romans 5:1-11).

Jesus, truly you are the Son of God! Give me the strength and vision to follow you and to minister to you, unto death!

COMMENT: Joseph of Arimathea, a pious Jew in search of the kingdom of God, asked for the crucified body of Jesus (v. 44). The details Mark gives about the time of this request (v. 42), the testimony of the centurion (v. 45), and the witness of the women at the burial (v. 47), surround the most important fact that Mark wishes to convey in this section: "Jesus was already dead" (repeated twice in v. 44). Mark's insistence on the reality of Jesus' death (the Greek word translated "body" in v. 45 is clearly "corpse") stands in stark contrast with the climax of Mark's Gospel: "You seek Jesus of Nazareth who was crucified. He has risen, he is not here" (16:6). He whose corpse was taken from the cross has been raised to life!

REFLECTION: Anyone who has lost a loved one can easily relate to this passage about the burial of Jesus. In the funeral parlor or at the gravesite there are those overwhelming feelings of "he/she is gone forever," much like Joseph and the women must have felt. More overwhelming still is the core Christian belief expressed by St. Paul: "Christ has been raised from the dead, the first fruits of those who have fallen asleep" (1 Cor 15:20). "Let us console one another with this message" (1 Thess 4:18).

Lord, I commend all of my deceased friends and relatives to your loving care. May I join them all one day, to be with you forever!

COMMENT: "And they said nothing to anyone, for they were afraid." So ends Mark's Gospel. Such an abrupt ending has caused scholars and believers to think that more was needed here. Since the 2nd century other endings (like vs. 9-20) have been added to Mark's own conclusion. However, by ending at v. 8 Mark has brought the Christian reader to the climax of his good news! "You thought Jesus was dead. He has risen, he is not here. See the empty tomb." How will Christians in Mark's day respond to the news? Will they join the ladies in trembling and astonishment? Will they even disobey God's inspired messenger by remaining silent, instead of proclaiming to the world that Christians believe in the one who brings life from death, who gives meaning to suffering, and who asks us to celebrate the life of the crucified and risen Jesus?

REFLECTION: An excellent film ends and the audience leaves the theater with the feelings desired by the director of the film. God's Word, as directed by Mark, is meant to inspire more than feelings. It leaves us with the challenge of living and of proclaiming our faith in the glorified Lord whom we do not see, but who waits for us where we shall see him, just as he told us!

Lord Jesus, make me as courageous and as intimate a follower of you as you made St. Mark. Proclaim your victory over suffering and death through me!

COMMENT: It comes as a shock to many new students of the Bible that scholars believe that vs. 9-20 are *not* a part of the Gospel of St. Mark. Although these verses were added to Mark's Gospel in the first or second century by another author, they have traditionally been accepted as the inspired Word of God. And so it is important to consider what God wants to say to us through them. The appearances of Jesus to Mary Magdalene (vs. 9-11) and to the disciples (vs. 12f. and 14-18) were added in order to inspire the early Church with some proofs and promises of the *risen* Lord (absent in Mark's conclusion, 16:1-8). The last section (vs. 19-20) gave second century Christians encouragement to continue to "go into all the world and preach the gospel to all creation" (v. 15).

REFLECTION: Nineteen hundred years after Mark wrote his "good news" about Jesus, we look around and find ourselves worthy of Jesus' rebuke in v. 14: "and he upbraided them for their unbelief and hardness of heart, because they had not believed those who saw him after he had risen." Perhaps our unbelief shows up most clearly when we give in to the frustration and discouragement that come with our Christian mission to renew the Church and the face of the earth. In hope we pray:

With men it is impossible, but not with God; for all things are possible with God. Lord, we leave all to follow you (Mk 10:27f.).

READ and PRAY SERIES

Edited By

ROBERT J. KARRIS O.F.M.

No. 1   GOSPEL OF ST. MATTHEW
by Donald Senior, C.P. .... .95c

No. 2   GOSPEL OF ST. LUKE
by Robert J. Karris O.F.M. .... .95c

No. 3   GOSPEL OF ST. JOHN
by Pheme Perkins .... .95c

No. 4   GOSPEL OF ST. MARK
by Philip Van Linden C.M. .... .95c

No. 5   ISAIAH
by Carroll Stuhlmueller C.P. .... .95c

No. 6   THE EPISTLE TO THE ROMANS
by Barnabas Ahern C.P. .... .95c

HERALD BIBLICAL BOOKLETS

General Editor, ROBERT J. KARRIS O.F.M.
Catholic Theological Union at Chicago

Glory and the Way of the Cross: Gospel of Mark
by Ludger Schenke, trans. by Prof. Robin Scroggs

The Formation of the Old Testament
by Joachim Becker, trans. by Dr. Walter Wifall

The Miracles of Jesus: Then and Now
by Alfons Weiser, trans. by Dr. David L. Tiede

The Gospels: God's Word in Human Words
by Gerhard Lohfink, trans. by William R. Poehlmann

Matthew: A Gospel for the Church
by Donald Senior C.P.

Following Jesus: A Guide to the Gospels
by Robert J. Karris O.F.M.

Faith in the Word: The Fourth Gospel
by George W. MacRae S.J.

Israel's Prophets: Envoys of the King
by Walter Wifall

Reconciliation: A Biblical Call
by Carroll Stuhlmueller C.P.

Covenant in the Old Testament
by Michael D. Guinan O.F.M.

The Faithful City
by Richard Sklba

Apocalypse
by Elisabeth Fiorenza

95¢ Each Title

— Other Titles in Preparation —

FRANCISCAN HERALD PRESS

1434 West 51st Street • Chicago, Illinois 60609